More Praise for *The Soulmaking Room*

Dee Dee Risher's inaugural book is beautiful, personal, and filled with spiritually grounded wisdom. She draws from her story to share how the difficult passages in our lives—the failures and losses—shape us into our best and most truthful selves.

—SHANE CLAIBORNE, Author, social activist, founding member of The Simple Way

What do you get when you cross an Anabaptist, a Pentecostal, and a mainline Protestant? The answer to that question is reason enough to read this book. Then add powerful meditations on failure, midlife, and building a woodshed out of the lumber of youthful dreams, and you have a book that warrants a term like *treasure*. I have long been a fan of Dee Dee Risher's work as an editor, first at *The Other Side* then at *Conspire*, but now in *The Soulmaking Room*, her own voice as a writer is being offered to the world—a gift and treasure indeed. This is truly beautiful writing and rich wisdom.

—BRIAN MCLAREN, Author and theologian

The bargain God offers the soul is simple but demanding: The price of enlightenment is that you are thus obligated to pass it on! Dee Dee Risher does that quite well—and she does it again here.

—RICHARD ROHR, Author of *Falling Upward* and other books; founder of Center for Contemplation and Action

Dee Dee Risher has spent her life engaged in the struggle for justice—as a poet, a singer, an editor, a mother, a friend. Deeply rooted in the biblical narrative, she has honed her craft of weaving together critical issues of race, class, oppression, the struggle to remain faithful, ric͏ ͏ ͏ ͏r-sonal stories from her life with her husband and tw͏ ͏ ͏ ͏t story of faith, and life in all its beauty and ͏ ͏ a work of art to help us see more clearl͏

—MURPHY DAVIS, Author, pastor, acti͏

I consider Dee Dee Risher one of our radicaі ͏ ͏ ͏ ͏ovement's most trustworthy, thoughtful, and compassionate ѕ͏ ͏ιs. Her journalism, prose, and poetry bear an authenticity and transparency that honors the dignity beneath our blemishes and finds faith amidst struggle. I commend her as an emerging elder helping us to embrace both Word and world.

—CHED MYERS, Theologian, author of *Binding the Strong Man* and other books, founder of Bartimaeus Institute

Dee Dee Risher brings to this book her usual combination of courage and eloquence. She moves back and forth between the witness of scripture and the truth she finds in her own life. The outcome of such interpretive work is that she can readily identify her life purpose and a force much larger than her own, the sort of thing that comes under the heading of "providence." Readers are invited by her book to reflect on their own lives in light of scripture. Her book is a welcome opportunity for thinking and praying again.

—WALTER BRUEGGEMANN, Theologian, author of *The Prophetic Imagination* and other books, Professor Emeritus of Old Testament, Columbia Theological Seminary

The things Dee Dee Risher said about gratitude—and said so well—brought my spirit back into focus. This is the kind of wisdom that we lose and have to rediscover at many points in life's journey. We can all be grateful for her faithful witness.

—DAVID JANZEN, Author and elder of Reba Place Fellowship

Dee Dee's book is cathartic for me: so honest, so refreshing, so helpful to have her articulate many of my experiences. It is incredibly well written—poetic and moving. I am astounded that she knows my interior life and doubts so well! She succeeded in something I didn't think was possible: capturing the intimate and honest feel of a letter to me, about me.

—ELIZABETH KILLOUGH, Director, Untours Foundation

In *The Soulmaking Room*, Risher writes beautifully, and her content is wise and profound. I am deeply grateful for her extended reflections on the story of the Shunammite woman, with its wonderful shamanic qualities.

—ROBERT ELLSBERG, Author and publisher, Orbis Books

THE
SOULMAKING
ROOM

DEE DEE RISHER

Blessings on your journey —
Dee Dee Risher

UPPER
ROOM BOOKS®
NASHVILLE

THE SOULMAKING ROOM
Copyright © 2016 by Dee Dee Risher
All rights reserved.

Upper Room Books® website: books.upperroom.org

Upper Room®, Upper Room Books®, and design logos are trademarks owned by The Upper Room®, Nashville, Tennessee. All rights reserved.

Scripture quotations not otherwise noted are from the New American Standard Bible®, Copyright © 1960, 1962, 1963, 1968, 1971, 1972, 1973,1975, 1977, 1995 by The Lockman Foundation Used by permission. www.Lockman.org.

Scripture quotations marked KJV are from the King James Version of the Bible.

"The Uses of Sorrow" from *Thirst* by Mary Oliver, published by Beacon Press, Boston. Copyright © 2004 by Mary Oliver, used herewith by permission of the Charlotte Sheedy Literary Agency, Inc.

"Once Only" by Denise Levertov, from *This Great Unknowing*, copyright © 1999 by The Denise Levertov Literary Trust, Paul A. Lacey and Valerie Trueblood Rapport, Co-Trustees. Reprinted by permission of New Directions Publishing Corp.

"The Art of Disappearing" from *Words Under the Words: Selected Poems* by Naomi Shihab Nye, copyright © 1995. Reprinted with permission of Far Corner Books.

Cover design: Jeff Miller | Faceout Studio
Interior design and typesetting: Kristin Goble | PerfecType

Library of Congress Cataloging-in-Publication Data

Names: Risher, Dee Dee.
Title: The soulmaking room / Dee Dee Risher.
Description: Nashville : Upper Room Books, 2016.
Identifiers: LCCN 2015032669| ISBN 9780835815253 (print) | ISBN
    9780835815345 (mobi) | ISBN 9780835815260 (epub)
Subjects: LCSH: Risher, Dee Dee. | Christian biography—United States. |
    Christian life.
Classification: LCC BR1725.R578 A3 2016 | DDC 277.3/083092—dc23
LC record available at http://lccn.loc.gov/2015032669

"We create ourselves by our choices."
Søren Kierkegaard

For all my people, who shaped me.

For Will, who has loved me relentlessly and believed in me when I did not.

And for Luke and Thea, whose faith in these words never wavered.

Contents

Foreword 9

Preface 13

The Ancient Story 17

Part I: Living Among My Own People

Chapter 1: Prophet, Woman, Holy Room 21

Chapter 2: Where My People Came From 27

Chapter 3: The Boat 36

Chapter 4: Faith of Our Forebears 44

Part II: Threshold and Door

Chapter 5: A Room for the Wayfarer 53

Chapter 6: Crossing the Border 57

Chapter 7: To Dream a World Beyond Race 64

Chapter 8: Life in the Red-Light District 71

Chapter 9: Crossing the Rubicon 80

Chapter 10: One Wild and Lovely Life 89

Part III: Of Gifts, Loss, and Persistence

Chapter 11: Tell Me Something Real 99

Chapter 12: The Woodshed of Grace 103

Chapter 13: Bed, Table, Lamp
Confessions on Marriage and Family I   112

Chapter 14: Parenting, Privilege, and Loss
Confessions on Marriage and Family II   119

Chapter 15: The Second Touch
Confessions on Race and Class I   129

Chapter 16: Raising Children Across the Divide
Confessions on Race and Class II   138

Chapter 17: This Reeling Earth
Confessions of a First-World Consumer I   148

Chapter 18: Who Will Save the Frogs?
Confessions of a First-World Consumer II   155

Part IV: Finding Our Own Face

Chapter 19: The Truth about Dreams   169

Chapter 20: One Light Burning   174

Chapter 21: Coming Home to Ourselves   180

Chapter 22: The Door of Authenticity   185

Chapter 23: Finding Shafts of Light   192

Chapter 24: Some New Face   197

Notes   208

Foreword

I first encountered Dee Dee Risher when she wrote a groundbreaking article about dozens of homeless families who were living in an abandoned cathedral and facing eviction. Her storytelling helped spark the fire that gave birth to The Simple Way, an intentional community in Philadelphia. And her passion for justice became part of the movement around those courageous mothers and children living in the abandoned church to prevent their eviction. That was twenty years ago.

Since then Dee Dee has become one of my closest friends. She is an artist of words—a poet. She tells stories with the ease of a mother in a rocking chair sipping sweet tea on the front porch. But the stories she tells are not fables and fairy tales; they are daring truth-tales of a faith that is not scared to dive into the darkness of its own doubts and questions. Her faith is not just about comforting the victims of injustice but also about driving a spike into the wheels of the machine that keeps running over people. While most Christians stay in the shallow end of the faith pool, Dee Dee invites you to wade in the water and get into the deep end where things are not as safe, not as crystal clear, and not as predictable. But the deep end is where the adventure happens.

Dee Dee Risher is a towering, strong woman with a tender heart, a contagious laugh, and a special eye for the overlooked and underappreciated. She reminds me a lot of Jesus; she has the same fire to flip tables and the same tears that flow for those who hurt.

Dee Dee was the wizard-editor of *The Other Side* magazine, which stretched the imagination of Christians during the culture wars of the 1980s and 1990s, pioneering conversations on race, sexuality, and politics that defied categories, transcended camps, and shattered stereotypes. This was long before many of us realized the "Moral Majority" might well be neither moral nor a majority. She insisted that Christians could talk about issues other than homosexuality and abortion before the rest of us knew that. After her work with *The Other Side*, Dee Dee helped launch and run *Conspire* magazine with me and my pals at The Simple Way. She is a legend in the movement for justice, peace, and equality. But not many people know her—until now.

Now you have Dee Dee's inaugural book, which appropriately is beautiful, personal, and filled with spiritually grounded wisdom. Dee Dee draws from her story to share how the difficult passages in our lives—the failures and losses—shape us into our best and most truthful selves. She frames these powerful insights around the story of the Shunammite woman who builds a holy room for God's prophet. In Dee Dee's hands, the story takes on a new life that speaks to the human experience.

As you will see, Dee Dee is a delightfully homegrown, all-organic, South Carolina woman who ended up in the sometimes-alien world of Duke University and a life of unusual choices. Along the way, her carefully crafted ideologies and theologies were blown away, freeing her up to discover a deeper, truer faith.

She has wrestled with the reality of white privilege when it does not feel like a privilege to have ancestors who were on the wrong side of history, slavery, and oppression. Like many of us, Dee Dee wishes that her relatives had been among those voices of dissent, but, alas, they were not. Nonetheless, the freedom movement found her.

One of the things you will discover as you read her book is that Dee Dee is wonderfully ordinary. She has certainly seen the world from her work in North Carolina to her time in China, but at the end of the day she is a mother, a courageous wife, a middle-aged freedom fighter who knows that most days of the revolution are far from spectacular. I think you, like me, will find yourself in her story. Our stories are gifts we share with one another and with the world. And when we share them, something magical happens. We remind each other that we are not alone as we heal from our wounds and as we dream of a better world. By sharing our own story, we help others write theirs. That is what Dee Dee Risher has done.

By honestly sharing herself with you, Dee Dee may very well help you find your truest self. Welcome to *The Soulmaking Room*.

—Shane Claiborne

Preface

A preacher friend of mine is fond of reminding me that every preacher has only one sermon, and each spends a lifetime lifting up that message. When I was younger, I found this dispiriting, as if we are all frustrated little mice constantly circling the same maze, deluding ourselves that we are making progress.

But as I have grown older, the image has become oddly comforting. It hints that we are each given a core reality to carry and incarnate. It implies that we all have a message that we alone are destined to give to the world. If we do not, that word will simply not go out. Suddenly the singleness of mind speaks to deep intentionality and discovery. Our job is to find our sermon and to speak it aloud. The whole concept rings of authenticity.

I wrote this book in an attempt to come home to my true self. It explores how the mixed experiences of our lives—and perhaps especially the most painful, difficult, and murky parts—allow us to become more authentic. They shape us into who we were intended to be.

This book is for people who have lived through stuff. It's for people who have carried big dreams but lately seem to find themselves mired in the ordinary business of living. Many of us have loved well—or loved poorly—and lost. We've had to look death in the eye more than once. Our tongues have encountered the metallic taste of failure.

When people ask me what I am doing now, I say I am writing a book. When they ask what it's about, I answer simply: "It's a midlife book." Sometimes I take a tentative step further. "It's a book about loss and . . . you know . . . failure. Failing at things we loved and wanted to thrive but didn't."

Silence.

I continue, "I'm trying to make failure teach me." I take a breath. "I think these failures may make me more myself, who I am supposed to be. Only I'm not sure I can figure it out."

I don't think I could have written this book until my midforties. For me, that was the time I was able to look closely at who I was, what I dreamed for the world, and, therefore, how I wished to shape and reshape my life. Such a passage can come at any time of life, but it often comes for the first time in our middle years.

My point of reevaluation was, predictably enough, prompted by several different parts of my life falling apart all at once—my job, my well-being, my sense of vocation and possibility. Many of the causes I cared about deeply faltered, stalled, and were co-opted by a crazy, self-indulgent, and affluent culture. I carried an inner staleness and the unsettling sense that I was oh-so-very imperceptibly becoming older and changing how I felt in my body. I'd arrived at all those midlife stereotypes at which society laughs. Yet if we are paying attention at all, we know each of us will have to grapple with large shifts in the flesh of our bodies and the configuration of our lives. We will have to reinvent ourselves.

Hidden in the beginning chapters of Second Kings is the story of a remarkable woman from Shunem. Her story showcases the power of a prophet; but, in fact, hers isn't actually a story about power or victory. From the underside, it is a story about mistakes, death, loss, and reshaping. Her story might contain all I know about the spiritual path.

And here's the funny thing: I started talking about this story—the story of a woman from Shunem—at a time when my own life was shaking on its old foundations, moaning for some new shape. And people listened. Some of them were total strangers. Tears came to their eyes, and they grabbed my hand in their own warm but trembling ones. And they started telling me their own stories—stories so authentic and vulnerable that I carried them inside like a fire, like a light. I had found a new kind of fellowship. I was not alone, and what went down in Shunem in that upper room was not a crazy story.

We can work toward healing this aching world in infinite ways. We can practice endless methods of prayer. We can experience a million different incarnations of living both grounded and just. But we cannot make that life authentically until we come home to ourselves. And that is sometimes a very long journey. So I start with stories—the story of that Shunammite woman, of the room she built, and of the holy man who sometimes came there. I share some of my own history as a way to remember how I grew into this life, this day. I remember—think again about my people, my tribe, my particular body—as a way to think about how we grow into our commitments, our dreams, and our yearnings.

English poet John Keats called this life a "vale of Soul-making." I love this image. It beautifully transforms that limp metaphor of life as a "vale of tears." No, life is a workshop; the crafting of our soul is our own work to do. We are all pieces of creation, of clay, into which we are asked to breathe life. It is ours to work that clay.

So here is my weave of history offered as reflection and witness. It contains scraps of scripture and those ancient stories that yearn to be told. I include passages from my journal, snippets from essays of passion I penned, and poetic jottings from the margins of my notebooks. I thank all those whose wisdoms speak to new lives. I have structured this book around some of the key turns in the story of the prophet Elisha and the woman of Shunem.

I wrote this book to come home. My deepest hope is that what I have written might join all that is inside you to bring you home to a deeper, more joyful, and patient knowing of yourself. May the storytelling here encourage you to tell your story. There are those in your life who need to hear it—and maybe not the shining and successful parts but rather the parts that are dark like earth and blind like tree roots growing through rock. These are the parts of your story that move you toward the light as you unfold your specific shape in the world.

The Ancient Story

Now there came a day when Elisha the prophet passed over to Shunem, where there was a prominent woman, and she persuaded him to eat food. And so it was, as often as he passed by, he turned in there to eat food. She said to her husband, "Behold now, I perceive that this is a holy man of God passing by us continually. Please, let us make a little walled upper chamber and let us set a bed for him there, and a table and a chair and a lampstand; and it shall be, when he comes to us, that he can turn in there."

One day he came there and turned in to the upper chamber and rested. Then he said to Gehazi, his servant, "Call this Shunammite." And when he had called her, she stood before him. He said to him, "Say now to her, 'Behold, you have been careful for us with all this care; what can I do for you? Would you be spoken for to the king or to the captain of the army?'" And she answered, "I live among my own people."

So he said, "What then is to be done for her?" And Gehazi answered, "Truly she has no son and her husband is old." He said, "Call her." When he had called her, she stood in the doorway. Then he said, "At this season next year you will embrace a son." And she said, "No, my lord, O man of God, do not lie to your maidservant."

The woman conceived and bore a son at that season the next year, as Elisha had said to her.

When the child was grown, the day came that he went out to his father to the reapers. He said to his father, "My head, my head." And he said to his servant, "Carry him to his mother." When he had taken him and brought him to his mother, he sat on her lap until noon, and then died. She went up and laid him on the bed of the man of God, and shut the door behind him and went out. Then she called to her husband and said, "Please send me one of the servants and one of the donkeys, that I may run to the man of God and return." He said, "Why will you go to him today? It is neither new moon nor sabbath."

And she said, "It will be well." Then she saddled a donkey and said to her servant, "Drive and go forward; do not slow down the pace for me unless I tell you." So she went and came to the man of God to Mount Carmel.

When the man of God saw her at a distance, he said to Gehazi his servant, "Behold, there is the Shunammite. Please run now to meet her and say to her, 'Is it well with you? Is it well with your husband? Is it well with the child?'" And she answered, "It is well." When she came to the man of God to the hill, she caught hold of his feet. And Gehazi came near to push her away; but the man of God said, "Let her alone, for her soul is troubled within her; and the LORD has hidden it from me and has not told me." Then she said, "Did I ask for a son from my lord? Did I not say, 'Do not deceive me'?"

Then he said to Gehazi, "Gird up your loins and take my staff in your hand, and go your way; if you meet any man, do not salute him, and if anyone salutes you, do not answer him; and lay my staff on the lad's face." The mother of the lad said, "As the LORD lives and as you yourself live, I will not leave you." And he arose and followed her. Then Gehazi passed on before them and laid the staff on the lad's face, but there was no sound or response. So he returned to meet him and told him, "The lad has not awakened."

When Elisha came into the house, behold the lad was dead and laid on his bed. So he entered and shut the door behind them both and prayed to the LORD. And he went up and lay on the child, and put his mouth on his mouth and his eyes on his eyes and his hands on his hands, and he stretched himself on him; and the flesh of the child became warm. Then he returned and walked in the house once back and forth, and went up and stretched himself on him; and the lad sneezed seven times and the lad opened his eyes. He called Gehazi and said, "Call this Shunammite." So he called her. And when she came in to him, he said, "Take up your son." Then she went in and fell at his feet and bowed herself to the ground, and she took up her son and went out.

2 Kings 4:8-37

PART I

Living Among My Own People

"I live among my own people."

2 Kings 4:13

How do I learn who my people are?

What treasure and what shadow have they proffered me?

Somewhere in the land between lie the quiet waters of
healing. I sit beside those waters. They bathe my hands, drink my
tears. They show me how to come home to myself.

Chapter 1

Prophet, Woman, Holy Room

The story begins with a yearning. An unnamed woman in the town of Shunem decides to build a room in her home for Elisha, the holy man. (Elisha is the prophet who carries the mantle after Elijah is swept up into a fiery chariot.) That act of hospitality changes her life.

> Now there came a day when Elisha passed over to Shunem, where there was a prominent woman, and she persuaded him to eat food. And so it was, as often as he passed by, he turned in there to eat food. She said to her husband, "Behold now, I perceive that this is a holy man of God passing by us continually. Please, let us make a little walled upper chamber and let us set a bed for him there, and a table and a chair and a lampstand; and it shall be, when he comes to us, that he can turn in there." One day, he came there and turned in to the upper chamber and rested (2 Kings 4:8-11).

Unlike most women in scripture, the Shunammite woman possesses some economic power. Just before she makes her appearance, scriptures record Elisha's miracles for a widow so poor that her two sons are about to be enslaved by creditors in payment for her meager debts. (See 2 Kings 4:1.) But no such threat of economic disaster plagues this prominent woman. She has resources, and she is persuasive. She has the ear of her spouse, presumably the real source of her economic power in a society where women have no wealth of their own. She convinces her husband to build an upper room for the prophet. It is a simple space—a small, walled chamber with a bed, table, chair, and lamp, open to him whenever he chooses to come. And he does come. The decision to build this space becomes an utterly life-changing act.

Acts of hospitality—giving or receiving—alter our lives forever. When we give our lives over to God and to the mystery of faith, we commit to building a room—right onto our own house, up against the sky. When any of us embark in earnest on a spiritual journey, we commit to the same. No pilgrimage is sustained without the creation of a holy room. Yet, creating such a space is extraordinarily difficult. In lives ridden with responsibilities, the tasks of daily maintenance, and the inertia of the ordinary, finding a creative and open place for soul work is not easy.

The ability to purchase space is perhaps the most powerful marker of affluence. I am sure many in Shunem would have shared their hospitality with the prophet but could not afford a guest room. Millions worldwide cannot even dream of a corner of a room. They share rooms with many others. They live in refugee camps. They live privately in our public spaces with no housing at all. Yet even in these settings we can find space that we can seize and make as an invitation to God.

We all have a space that the Holy One is waiting to enter—a crack through which the Spirit can slip. Once, while walking the mobbed streets of Beijing, pushed on every side, I almost tripped over a monk seated cross-legged on the sidewalk in deep, unwavering meditation. He was completely oblivious to the teeming school of pedestrians swimming around him. He had left that crowd to walk in the quiet places.

The Shunammite simply says to the prophet: "I would like to open my door to your life, to your comings and goings." This is much more vulnerable than a one-time offer of housing or a scheduled visit. Later, Jesus gives us an image of the Spirit of God as a wayward wind, blowing through as it wishes, from the unknown toward the unknown. God comes, bidden or unbidden. So she builds a room. The prophet begins to stay in the room. And the story unfolds in all its beauty and grief.

The prophet wishes to give the Shunammite woman something in return for her hospitality.

> Then [Elisha] said to Gehazi his servant, "Call this Shunam-mite." And when he had called her, she stood before him. He said to him, "Say now to her, 'Behold, you have been careful for us with all this care; what can I do for you? Would you be spoken for to the king or to the captain of the army?' " And she answered, "I live among my own people" (2 Kings 4:12-13).

We just can't get away from the idea of spiritual rewards. It runs through scripture, teachings, and theology. It embodies our constructs of heaven and hell, and we use those perceptions as our ultimate motivator. We reward devotion—*Believe in me and I will reward you.* But a flip side exists as well—*Don't believe in me and I will punish.* So we shouldn't be surprised that Elisha, the holy man, soon poses a question to the Shunammite woman: "What can I do for you?"

What can I do for you? Should we be offered a prize for the sacrifice of belief? Something is wrong with the expectation or premise that we pursue a life of faith for reward or justification. Do we follow the faith or spiritual discipline because it is a richer, more empowering, and thoughtful way to walk this human path? Or do we expect some economic gain, some foot up the ladder because of our faithfulness? The question we need from the Holy One is different, more searching. *What can I offer you that matches the yearning of your heart?*

We want life to be a meritocracy where people earn what they receive. We want people to get their just deserts. And a great deal of scripture devotes itself to exactly that premise. Personally, I want some sorting out, some vindication for all my life choices. I want humanity to be rewarded for some actions; I want other lessons (finally) pounded into the heads of all the errant and greedy waywards.

Like everyone else, I want to sit at the heavenly banquet table Isaiah speaks of, where everyone at last sits down together. Many days, I want everyone to be there. On less generous days, I have a list of folks who should be scolded and told to stay in the kitchen and clean up.

Perhaps we should consider the idea of reward from a totally different angle. The real teaching of the Shunammite woman's story is that if we cultivate a holy life—if we host the Holy One—fruits will follow. These fruits serve as a natural and organic outcome of the discipline of love and attentiveness.

Elisha, however, seems to have something more worldly in mind. He seems, in fact, to be one of those prophets who has cultivated the ear of the powerful—and so, perhaps, is worthy of our skepticism. He offers to put in a good word with the king or the head of the army. This is no Jeremiah wearing a nasty, ragged loincloth in the wilderness. Elisha keeps company with those of worldly influence.

I love the way this Shunammite woman acts upon her suspicion of Elisha's offer. Reward had not occurred to her, and she shows no interest in one. And so she speaks the beautiful response, "I live among my own people" (2 Kings 4:13). Her grounded answer comes from her willingness to know herself and where she comes from. Her words embody the certainty of blessing and birthright. *I am already blessed. I have enough. No, holy man, I need nothing from you.*

Who are my people? The work of becoming the person I was created to be began with that single question; yet answering it has taken decades. Sometimes I feel it will take my entire life. I was raised in a world that focused on individual moral failures and shortcomings. It was neither discerning of nor willing to acknowledge social identity. People were disinterested in exploring how race, class, gender, and cultural background affected their assumptions or perceptions of the world and of faith itself. Ultimately, those around me did not believe that such factors were relevant in a faith conversion because true conversion was supposed to erase those differences. To give such factors too much import somehow diminished the power of God to overcome all barriers.

Yet I believe that we are able to speak across lines of difference only when we have been unrelentingly honest and specific about whom we have been created to be, both as individuals and as part of a social class. We must know our own people and live among them. So it is important for me to name and unravel my varied identities—Christian, female, white, North American, from the southern United States, heterosexual, with parents from upper-middle- and working-class backgrounds. These factors shape the lenses through which I view life. They are not determinate, but they are influential. I may reflect some common behaviors of one socioeconomic group and not others, but they remain powerful—and usually unexamined—forces shaping how I see the world, how I read the Word of God, and how I understand the teachings of Jesus. To dismiss them as labels irrelevant to my life would be a delusion.

I've spent a lot of time trying to understand how these sociocultural realities have impacted how I see the world—thinking about how I became "white," what class means for me, what being a woman means to me and how it changes my experience of the world, how being a parent changes me, how my Southernness changes me.

I'm trying to understand and live among my own people.

I once had the pleasure of talking with Dr. Ysaye Barnwell, the fabulous bass voice in the stunning a cappella group Sweet Honey in the Rock, about her life as a singer, and she told me a story about the power of living among one's own people.

Dr. Barnwell wrote a song called "No Mirrors in My Nana's House," which is really about unconditional love. Her lyrics celebrate that her grandmother's house had no mirrors to reflect the judgments of the world, and so she felt both loved and beautiful. "There were no mirrors in my Nana's house / no mirrors in my Nana's house / and the beauty that I saw in everything / was in her eyes (like the rising of the sun). / I never knew that my skin was too black. / I never knew that my nose was too flat. / I never knew my clothes didn't fit. / I never knew there were things that I missed, / 'cause the beauty in everything was in her eyes."[1]

Dr. Barnwell spoke about what the response to that song taught her:

I have learned that the more specific we can be, the more universal we are. At the core, we all share something. When I get specific, I am getting closer to that core. I no longer try to appeal to everything out there. I go deeper inside myself. . . . This is the only way I can account for reactions to a song like "No Mirrors." . . . I could not be more specific about my own pain around how I look than to put into a song that my nose is broad, and I am black. That experience is so specific to my growing up, so painful. . . . And yet we sing that verse, and I see White women on the front row crying. We sing that song, and I get letters from White gay male ensembles who want to sing that song because they see in it unconditional love. The deeper I go, the more general I become. It's a paradox—but it's true.[2]

I find tremendous hope in the truth Dr. Barnwell offers. Often group identity is accompanied by a clear sense of who does not belong in the group. This is the difficult side of community. So Dr. Barnwell's intuition that our true, lived diversity comes from embracing our particularities lifts my heart. Authentic diversity comes from recognizing and deeply embracing our own particular identities rather than denying them. We begin by naming our people in all their complexity, embracing them, and then releasing parts of them in order to grow. We name our people to recognize and venture beyond the mold they gave us. When we venture away from our people, we will find that we travel home by a different way and return changed.

Chapter 2

Where My People Came From

My childhood was painted on a backdrop of land, sky, and water. My family lived eight miles outside the town limits next to a lonely, small-town airstrip in a not-happening corner of a rural county. There was lots of open land to roam, and it was a time when parents felt okay about kids roaming by themselves.

After school and homework, my sisters and I were left to explore the land around our house. Even in winter, the Southern sun was long and kind. I remember roving the forests, gullies, small drainage creeks, and pastures—sometimes alone, sometimes accompanied by my sisters and neighbor playmates. We were fierce and relentless pioneers. We played "old timey days." We built endless tree houses and named every corner of the area—"Magic Mountain," "Mossy Swamp," "The Gumball Tree," "The Secret Place." I read books in trees, wrote essays crouched in gullies.

I experienced seemingly the best of childhoods. My parents were hardworking, loving, and involved with my family even as they built a school. My sisters and I were close, and we had an endless world in which to play. Because my parents worked at a school, summers always had a more open rhythm. My family was not idyllic, but it was functional. Things got done. Kids got fed, got to school, went to church, grew up. My parents valued education, and being the children of parents and grandparents who went to college, my sisters and I were expected to go to college. We all went. Like all families, mine was composed of characters with their share of bullheadedness, brokenness, and quirks, and we have grown to adulthood with our share of hurts and wounds. My elderly friend pokes fun. "Oh, yeah, you're the generation that reads parenting books!" I laugh, but he is right. Most of my peers—other parents—are quite intentional. We think about how to raise our kids.

Such introspection and psychological analysis was not a currency of my household growing up, nor did my parents focus inordinately upon my sisters and me. My mother's primary value in the rearing of children was to train each of us to be independent at an early age. With a family of five children born in seven years and a new family business to launch, this was a sensible goal. Though I remember short, one-year incursions into a few extracurricular classes (ballet and Brownies among them) we were not allowed to participate in any after-school activities until we could manage our own transportation there and home again. My mother did not plan to spend afternoons carting kids around, nor did her shifting pool of odd jobs at the fledgling school allow it.

The one exception to my mother's ban on extracurricular activities was piano lessons. My father and his family felt strongly about music. All five of us dutifully took lessons, and when I was six and my parents moved into a two-story house they built next to the school's campus, the small, brown spinet in the corner of the living room was replaced by an elegant baby grand.

At night after work, my father would sit in the living room and listen to music on his turntable. I would sometimes creep in and watch him. He sat, totally unaware of my presence, often with eyes closed, tapping rhythms on his knee and nodding his head. For everyone else in my life, music, if present at all, was a background noise you turned on while you did other things. I was arrested by my father's focus on the music itself. He loved the classics—especially Tchaikovsky, Beethoven, Chopin—and music poured from the light-drenched room through open windows to the back lawn, the pine woods, and the darkened pasture beyond.

Thriftiness undergirded by basic economic security cushioned my childhood. My mother's farming family did not believe in paying anyone else to come in and do what you could do yourself ("Or thought you *might* be able to do," my father would quip). So she would hire assistance in extreme circumstances, but she worked right alongside. She never had any function catered, even those attended by hundreds of people. She sewed our clothes (expertly), cut our hair (inexpertly), grew some of our food, and took tremendous pleasure in bargains and small frugalities. "The only thing I can say is that your father's family must have hailed from royalty the way they like to hire other people to do their work," my mother would proclaim.

This was true. My dad was a supervisor type and backed this tendency with an economic rationale. He saw his role as administering a school. He was not a farmer, and he did not pick strawberries (or build furniture, tend the garden, do home repairs, and so on). In his opinion, the economic model worked only because he respected this division of labor and hired a person to pick strawberries instead of picking his own. If he were too much of a do-it-yourselfer, he argued (a bit tongue-in-cheek), an economic crash would ensue. I absorbed these subtle perspectives on class—and the lifestyles spawned by them—unconsciously.

When my parents were young, most everyone farmed or was only one generation out from doing it. My father's family had made the jump to town when my grandfather left the family farm to teach, and he subsequently ran a boarding "finishing school"—later military academy—in the small town of Bamberg, South Carolina. My mother's family still farms outside Cameron, South Carolina, a small community that retains the basics—gas station, church, barbeque pit. My maternal uncles were among the few farmers scattered all over South Carolina who successfully transitioned from small-scale, multicrop farming to agribusiness, growing soybeans, cotton, and corn—a totally different venture than the small-scale farming of my mother's childhood.

My parents moved one hour—and a whole world—up the road to Camden, South Carolina, a small town located in the central sand hills. What was once a shoreline offered some of the poorest, sandiest soil in the Southeast, suitable only for blackjack and scrub oak, long-leaf pine, and broom-straw grasses. It was not lovely land, but we find ways to love the land that is our home, and I did.

Contrary to my mom's jibe, my paternal grandmother's family was not nobility. Though they were the wealthiest branch of our family, they weren't even particularly well-off monetarily. My grandmother had lost her father to the kick of a bull when she was very young. Her scrappy mother, Ida Mae Folk Varn, raised her and her five siblings alone. The oldest boys left home to support the family before they were fifteen years old and did so handsomely. Yet members of that side of the family possessed the wealth the agrarian South valued—land and human beings. A great-great-uncle on that Folk side is recorded in the 1800s as possessing more than one hundred slaves, which would have made him a wealthy man. The mahogany bed in my grandparent's house, so high I had to use a footstool to climb atop it and hear Gaga's stories, was crafted by slaves.

These haunting realities were mentioned somewhat matter-of-factly in my growing up years. How that land and slave wealth, even diluted by generations, helped a poor widow sustain her family did not become part of family lore in the way that those enterprising young brothers who worked their way into banks and car dealerships did. It was, in fact, the resources from my paternal grandmother's family that really enabled my grandfather, James Risher, to buy and build the family business. He grew up the oldest son of unschooled parents. Though he never went to high school, he taught himself well enough on his own to apply for and receive a scholarship to attend college at the Citadel. This nailed him the credentials he needed to become a one-room schoolteacher and later to teach at a boarding school.

My grandfather was still a fairly young man when he decided to buy the boarding school where he worked and make it a military secondary school. Running military schools became the odd family business. That first school, Carlisle, became so successful that my grandfather opened another school in Camden. He installed my father as the headmaster, guiding the entire process carefully as he groomed my father for the work. My father was twenty-six, and that was the year I was born.

My father worked consuming hours all year, building the school with my mother's full partnership. My grandfather's significant experience guided him through the most precarious decisions. In those early years, I only remember seeing my father at home for late-night, right-before-bed gambols. He would appear in the small apartment that our family had on the school campus after supper and baths to scoop us up. We took turns crawling up the red leather hassock in our den in our soft flannel nightgowns. He lay flat on his back below us, arms outstretched to grab us under the arms, flip us over his head, and land us, hooting like bandits, between his lanky, sprawling legs. But his life was clearly elsewhere, consumed by the school and the immense responsibilities he had shouldered.

Summer seemed an endless continuation of our tribe-centered family life, with the addition of long family trips to the South Carolina coast or the mountains of North Carolina (mostly minus my father, who stayed home, worrying about school enrollment and making arrangements for the upcoming school year). My farming uncles and maternal grandfather worked one summer to build a small cabin on a beautiful mountain stream near Asheville, North Carolina, and we usually spent a few weeks there during the summer immersed in the magical world of cousins—exploring the stream by day, playing slap-jack and rummy all night, whispering to one another until we fell asleep in the attic loft long past our bedtimes.

My family also spent weeks at the beach. Hurricane Hazel leveled the South Carolina coast in the midfifties, and my mother's savvy, deal-wielding farmer-father convinced my father to take advantage of bargain-basement beach real-estate prices and purchase a small duplex. He paid about seven thousand dollars for the beach house and lot. We christened it the Turtle Egg, even though beach development was starting to ensure that no turtle eggs would be laid at that beach again. We spent three weeks of our summer there and rented it out the rest of the time.

The house contained three small, thin-paneled bedrooms and two tiny baths in the upstairs apartment where we stayed, with an identical apartment below. Usually our time there was shared with relatives and grandparents. When my grandmother was there, she slept in the room with me and one of my sisters. Grandmama and I would rise early, she would have her coffee, and then we would leave my sisters and parents curled under flimsy cotton spreads that lifted slightly with their breathing, rhythmically like the roll of the waves outside.

Grandmama and I would pad down the steps and into the damp sand, smoothed and flattened since the day before, all tracks of sandcastles, dogs, and Frisbees erased. Grandmama never missed anything. She pointed out clouds with just a certain tinge of rose against the blue expanse of sky, the colors of the sea oats against the dunes, the way the sea had weathered a particular piece of driftwood, the flash of purple hidden in a shell. It was as though she curated a museum of mysteries. Only when she pointed them out did I see the miracles—the brilliant color, the artistry of each canvas.

We were serious shell hunters, Grandmama and I. She complimented me on my eagle eye, so I trained myself to focus on the banks of shells that dotted the beach, to discriminate immediately the colors and shapes that held "value." Value was determined by unspoken rules. Shells that were unusual variations on coloring were deemed valuable, as was colored glass frosted opaque by the sand, seaweed that kept its color, sea animals washed on shore, and fragile shapes that had survived the seething waters—crab shells, pin shells, sand dollars. Anything that was still living—sea urchins, hairy sand dollars, starfish—was admired and returned to the unforgiving ocean. Grandmama pointed to things that caught her eye with her cane. I picked them up for her, and in return, she taught me to call them by name and told me about their lives in the sea. Upon our return to the house, Mom would be cooking breakfast; a few sisters would be awake. Grandmama took her coffee on the porch, rocking, rocking all morning, watching the ocean change colors for her like an old, old friend.

Months later, after a Thanksgiving or Christmas dinner held at Grandmama's farm, I would slip away from tables laden with ham, turkey, oyster pie, green Jell-O salad, and banana pudding. Flushed with the mix of heavy food, a roaring fire, and excitement of family, I would open the door of the unheated, enclosed back porch off the kitchen. The cold air smelled faintly of detergent and dog food. Captured in blue-tinted Mason jars were our shells. The best of our summer trophies were now sorted and stacked on shelves—jingles and conchs and pin shells, keyholes and the olive roller shells my grandfather fashioned into neckties, ruby scallop shells, and razor clams. They sat waiting, memory and promise at once, looking out over the stubble fields and the bare trees with the detachment of resigned exiles. I drew a large conch to my ear and heard the ocean, rolling and churning. It sang the cadence of my childhood: "Love this world of miracle and beauty."

I had few early experiences that would make me a defector from the world in which I was raised. I grew up oblivious of how social class affected my life and choices. My development followed a fairly typical trajectory. When we are children, we spend our time trying to make sense of basic relationships—what our parents want from us, how we relate to our siblings, and how we fit into our families. Like most kids, I explored what I was good at, whether people liked or hated me, and whether I was funny. Only much later did I became conscious of the broad differences in group behaviors and aesthetics that come with social class. Slowly I would begin to sense how my background affected subtle social markers like how I used language or related to the economic and political system, how I arranged my home, or how I raised my family.

Many wealthy families resided in Camden, South Carolina. It was the home of a world-renowned steeplechase, and the horse circuit is a profitable one. Affluent families from the Northeast also chose Camden as a site for their winter refuge. But my sisters and I were largely oblivious of wealth and its distinctions. We did not live in town but in the "unincorporated rural outlying areas." We spent our childhoods running around the woods and fields, not thinking twice about our crooked pageboy haircuts and our homemade, hand-me-down clothing. My mother's rural grounding and my parents' move to a town in which they were not part of the social network kept our childhood mostly free of social expectations. We never felt any scarcity, and economic strain did not weave itself into my parents' marriage. Yet with my parents totally preoccupied with a young family and building a new business (we often referred to the school as "the firstborn"), we escaped the indulgence and intense social awareness fostered by privilege, while we also absorbed few of the insecurities and tense emotions of scarcity. The land and space we lived in largely insulated us from the subtle class issues of America, fluid and shifting as they were. Any class consciousness would come much, much later.

In Annette Lareau's fascinating work on class and the raising of children, *Unequal Childhoods: Class, Race, and Family Life*, she points out that the current intense cultivation of our children is a definitive cultural shift—a modern phenomenon influenced by having more disposable income and social attentiveness. Increasingly, middle- and upper-middle-class children have highly structured lives—team sports, training in dance or music, playdates. Many travel to foreign countries at an early age. In contrast, parents with strong working-class roots raise their children with more unstructured time where family and neighborhood networks are paramount. There is precious little structured activity. Children monitor themselves; parents intervene primarily in the case of riot or injury.[1] (A friend of mine quips, "You know, free-range children.")

That's it, I think. *Free-range* is what my sisters and I were on those long afternoons in the woods, along mountain streams, and on the coast of my childhood. From my parents' time to my own, parenting has shifted completely. We moved from laissez-faire parenting—where the primary parental responsibilities were feeding, clothing, and getting kids to the local school—to more proactive, intentional, and resource-sucking enrichment. My parents did not think about predators or who would get us in the woods behind our house. But I raise my children in a different world, a world more complicated and hostile and infused with intense materialism.

When I was eight, my father's parents gave my family an extravagant gift. A truck pulled up at the door of our new house, and a heavy box was hauled in. Inside was a color television, and it was duly installed in the family den. My mother felt deep skepticism about the television and did not want this one. (We had a small black-and white set that we had unexpectedly won in a raffle, much to my mother's chagrin. Prior to the delivery of the color TV, I have no memory of it being turned on.) Television in my childhood was a rationed quantity—we watched thirty minutes a day max. Mom turned off the TV every chance she got.

But once that technology was ushered into our living space, we could not keep the world at bay. The TV brought the world into our home, some truth as well as a lot of fictions, distortions, and stereotypes. Within a year of its arrival, that TV would pipe in assassinations, race riots, and massive war protests. It would usher into our family room self-absorbed soap operas, ripe with sexual peccadilloes and deceit and greed. It would, very slowly, begin to teach us about the rich, the poor, and the middle class, and most of those teachings would not be true. That television symbolized and launched the screen age in which parents were much less able to protect their children from being shaped by unwanted external social forces. Soon the introduction of Internet and cell phones would make more clear how elusive and illusionary is any sense of parental control over the environment of our children.

The world was turning—had already turned for good and for bad. There was no looking back.

Chapter 3

The Boat

One of my most secure childhood memories is of family trips "back home." My parents, four sisters, and I piled into our blue Plymouth station wagon for the hour-long drive through South Carolina fields and swampland to the farm where my mother grew up. We'd sing our way around winding Highway 601, first through stands of lumbered pine forest, then by pastureland and small country churches, shacks and a sprinkling of small towns until we rolled into those communities my parents called home.

Most of my family, paternal and maternal, grew up in the South Carolina low country in rural communities around Orangeburg, Calhoun, and Bamberg counties. On my maternal grandfather's farm, I would see aunts, uncles, and a tribe of cousins. We spent endless afternoons fishing or hiding in snowy fields of cotton, sliding down heaps of soybeans, and playing games of kick-the-can well into the night. Lying in the bed in which my great-grandfather had died, I would listen to the whippoorwill across the back pond.

Then my parents would drive my sisters and me thirty more miles through country roads to my father's sleepy hometown where more aunts, uncles, and cousins lived in neighborhoods marked by churches, small storefronts, azaleas, and towering live oaks. We'd return to our house at night, often with an evening thunderstorm pattering on the roof. The soft suede of my dad's jacket under my cheek and the sway of the heavy Plymouth lulled me to sleep. I had nothing to fear.

My sisters and I memorized the journey with little stories about the places we saw along the way. We spoke of the haunted house that neighbors swore had been rolled to its current site from the banks of the Congaree River one mile away. We noticed the abandoned auto body shop in the middle of nowhere between a swamp and a field, a faded yellow racecar hoisted up on a big metal pole. There was the gas station and backroom arcade where Mom and I searched out the owner of a flock of peacocks we saw feeding by the road. (It was September, and we wanted feathers.) We passed the Congaree Swamp, virgin timbers towering over the still, black water, then the railroad tracks and that green copse that marked the swimming hole where my mother learned to swim. Now I hurtle my children home via interstates, passing exits that we remember vaguely by outlet mall, gas stations, and fast-food restaurants.

I wonder if thirty years ago my parents were already afraid of what I was too young to imagine: the dismantling of the world they knew—a world marked by extended kinship and specific place—was well underway. The Plymouth fueled by cheap gas, the roads on which it carried us, the large-scale farm equipment we climbed on, the familiar store chains in fledgling malls we pointed out as we sped along the highway—all stood as hallmarks of the world I would grow into. Perhaps only because I lived in rural South Carolina backwaters, where change comes slow, was I able to know the other, former world at all.

Today, living in the urban center of an aging superpower nation, these memories serve as an emotional touchstone that ground me in land, community, and family. In contrast, the world in which my generation is making its adult mark is characterized by conspicuous consumption, isolation, and fear. We fear for our jobs, our health, and our future. We fear for our children who grow up in unprecedented exposure to violence, constant entertainment, and materialism. The cultural forces of globalism and monoculture are subtly erasing place and its distinctive features. Anything can hail from everywhere. The face of commercial districts in Dallas, Savannah, Spokane, Juneau, and Bangor are identical. None of their products come from there. We can shop everywhere and feel like we are shopping anywhere. As we engage in economic transactions outside our neighborhoods, communities, and relationships, we increasingly live in ways that consume rather than sustain balance. We do this in an age where technology brings any reality, bidden or unbidden, to our dancing fingertips. Technology has in many ways erased the constraints of geography, and with that, some of its accompanying richness.

Even more distressing, predictions of environmental devastation and apocalypse come with the morning paper. Vast populations across the globe are uprooted by storms, global economic shifts, and ethnic and religious violence. Many religious ideologies simply feed a violent hostility toward others. People clamor at the borders of the United States for refuge. They point to wasteful lifestyles and an economy built on exploitation, reminding us that our way of life is neither permanent nor just.

I watched these cultural phenomena unfold in my hometown of Camden (population ten thousand) during my childhood. It began with Lowe's breathing down the neck of Moultrie Burns Hardware Store, with OfficeMax casting its long shadow over Blake and Ford, and with Food Lion sidling up to the Camden Food Shop and whispering, "My apples are bigger than your apples." Camden's main streets grew quiet, and the sprawling strip malls on the outskirts of town proliferated. Then Walmart got the brilliant idea that it could skulk on the peripheries of small towns and become a downtown district all by itself—grocery, bank, hardware store, and pharmacy. The Walmart revolution, a memorable blow for global capitalism, sucked my town—and many others—inside out. The view of the landscape from the tailgate of that old Plymouth station wagon would soon change entirely.

But I grew up in a rural South Carolina that still had a vibrant sense of place—a sense that included smell, sight, sound, color, and taste. People wanted to know where you were from and who your people were. My elders believed that the best the world had to offer was right around here—not only the best butter beans but also the world's smartest doctors, the most talented teachers, the best writers. I was raised in a world where people still sent you home with signature foods because certain foods were regional specialties you would not be able to get "up the road." I don't love sweet potatoes, but in my adult life, I have dutifully carried bags of them back to wherever I lived at the time because my parents know no one's sweet potatoes are cured better than Mr. Truesdale's. My frugal mother has spent fortunes to mail me the first-picked McBee peaches packed carefully in foam. Christmas booty always includes pecans from the farm, the best country ham, and fruitcake made from my grandmother's recipe. I don't even like fruitcake, but I can eat that kind of fruitcake all day. I'm grateful that I lived in a little backwater area where the tidal waters came in a little later and allowed me—a blade of small, green, new grass—to take root before they arrived.

But if the South of my childhood gave me a sense of rootedness, my people also gave me legacies of injustice that will take lifetimes to unravel. I was a white kid, not even ten, when all those dreams burned to the ground in 1968. I was riding the school bus to fourth grade, sitting by the window with the sun in my eyes, when a big kid in the aisle (white, of course—all the kids in my public school then were white) mentioned, rather matter-of-factly, that someone named Martin Luther King Jr. had been shot the night before. I was confused. I was a good Lutheran, and I was sure that the only Martin Luther I ever heard of had died a long time ago.

My utter lack of knowledge has always been a deep lesson to me about the insularity of race. As a white kid, I knew absolutely nothing about one of the greatest and most historical movements in recent history, a movement that unfolded in my own backyard. I don't think my parents actively shielded me from it, but I didn't need to be. The racial distance already there simply bore its unconscious fruits. The next year, a boy named George joined my fifth grade and became the first African American student ever to be in my classroom. He sat two desks over from me. I remember him as being a little funny, always ready to be the clown. I was polite, but I did not make a special effort to befriend him.

Any child growing up in the South soon hit the invisible lines of racial control, with all its attached and unstated codes. I could resist these codes or accede to them, but it was impossible to remain oblivious. Every person who has come out on the other side has stories of the moment the scales fell off the eyes, and normal no longer seemed normal or easy.

As an adult, I have listened to many white people excavating their relationship to race in this country by describing their first encounter with an African American person. In the South of my childhood, this would be like trying to remember the first time you saw daylight or the moon. The lives of blacks and whites were entwined in surreal ways on a daily basis. As an adult, I've been struck with the distance between racial groups in other parts of the county, a cross-racial distance that is foreign to me.

My mother called me while I was parenting two young children, and I heard her sigh over the phone as she said, "I don't know how you do it." My mom is a dynamo. I would put her right up there against the folk hero John Henry. She is from a family of farmers who work dawn to dusk. They have built their houses and the furniture in them. They make their clothes and put up vast quantities of food. My uncles repair their machines, and the best gift you can give them is to ask them to do two things at one time instead of one.

"Mom, you raised five kids whose ages spanned seven years," I countered.

"Oh, but I had help."

Help. I remember these women from my childhood and adulthood, women toward whom I followed custom and called by their first names without the requisite Southern "Miss" as preface. When I was older, this was uncomfortable, but these women came into my life at childhood when I had no way to mediate social disparities, custom, and power. They came and did whatever needed to be done, mostly alongside my mom—changing babies, washing, hanging laundry, cooking. I remember Merlene's melodious tones and soft voice, the way she showed me how to fold my clothes, and how she knew I loved that white straw purse with the purple flowers on top. I remember how I felt victory when I got Hannah, an extremely quiet woman, to suddenly burst out in laughter, and how precisely because she was practically the only quiet person in my loquacious house, I would attentively listen to any terse sentence from her mouth. These women corrected and scolded my sisters and me as needed, and they seemed glad to see us when we returned home from college.

Black domestic workers in white homes knew the intimacies of white lives with startling familiarity: how we talked to each other in an argument, where we kept our underwear, what we said to best friends on the phone. White people, on the other hand, knew little or almost nothing about the lives of these men and women they spent their days around.

Every human interaction across racial lines was mediated by these realities of power and place. Although I knew the names of Hannah's sons and how old they were, I never met them. Some of my family's maids drove to my home, but most got rides from people I never talked to, or my parents drove them to a part of town where their ride picked them up. (Hannah lived in the country; I never visited her home. Only when her mother died and she moved into a house in town did I ever visit her in her own place.)

Relationships between whites and blacks were like looking in a one-way mirror. Like many relationships that we create across lines of economic necessity, there was no reciprocity in the relationships and no desire for it. For blacks, this distance was a necessary protection and a legacy of slavery and Jim Crow. Blacks and whites lived with eerie, false relationships. They could all be as close as they wished to be in the day, but at night, both had to be on their side of the tracks. Even as I write about the family "help," I walk through land mines of stereotypes. It's hard to discuss race in America without talking in broad brushstrokes of stereotype and caricature. There is no other ground to talk about something as complex, nuanced, and subtle as race in this country.

To be certain, these relationships were distorted by racism, historical oppression, and privilege. They also included complexities and ironies of class. My mom had help so that she could leave her five children and work, and she did not go to white-collar, professional jobs. She was planting shrubbery on the campus of my father's school. She was working in the kitchen of the school and running a small canteen on campus. She was not hosting luncheons, overseeing a fancy household, or going to social gatherings. Even still, my mother had the resources to equip her household when she couldn't be there, and that fact alone showed her privilege.

My mother still sees the women she hired to work in her home over the years. Now that Hannah is homebound by a stroke, she stops over pretty regularly to talk or to see if she needs something and to give her any family news. In Hannah's living room, photos my sisters and I have sent of our families are stuck in the corner of some of the many picture frames. Extricating the true relational aspect from the structured economic relationship of oppression and privilege is impossible.

All this said, I believe whites commonly presumed an intimacy and familiarity with the African Americans who worked with and around them that was not reciprocated. Years later, my mentor Margaret, who worked as a domestic for years in the home of Janice, a white woman, once told me that Janice's daughter, home from college, would sometimes phone and ask to see her. She might agree. She might not. Margaret was a fixture in that white home, but she always felt separate, alien, and detached. It was a place where she was never herself. Meanwhile, white people felt trust in some goodwill from the blacks to whom they were connected in spite of the broader historical weight of exploitation, humiliation, and murder.

Black and white, poor and working, middle and upper class—we were stepping into historical legacies much larger than ourselves. These were the social dynamics into which I was inducted at birth, cast into a role by skin color. We all were. I was never truly successful at undermining the code in the community in which I grew up, though I found that I was able to in other places. One of the social codes it took several years for me to notice was the "not front door" rule that applied to both black and white workers not in professional, white-collar roles. Another was that the "help" ate alone after the family. The sight of Hannah eating in solitude after my family had eaten filled me with discomfort and shame, a kind of breached hospitality. When I was older, I tried to eat with her a few times, but our conversation was labored, and she looked out the window as she silently chewed her food. I realized I was making her uncomfortable and probably taking away the single half hour of peace in her day when she could be mentally removed from our house and us. I stopped. I wanted to start calling her Ms. Perkins, using her last name, as I now called other African American women, but it was too awkward and did not communicate the respect I wished to evoke. These small and ultimately ineffective rebellions seemed to embarrass all parties.

The way the humanity in people tolerated this caste system was to follow the patterns without thinking—not breaking the pattern allows us not to think about it. One did not rock the boat. But thankfully, it was the late sixties, and there were hands everywhere reaching from the water, grabbing that little, shaky skiff, rocking it hard.

Chapter 4

Faith of Our Forebears

On a late November afternoon in Beijing, the cold fell fast. I was walking with Xiao Zhang, a seventeen-year-old student. She was the most intelligent student in my class, and her acerbic delivery and severe, cat-eye glasses hinted at a young woman with quick, sure, and definite opinions. She always laughed one beat late, as though she realized she was supposed to but was not really amused.

That night Xiao Zhang was focused on understanding the superstitions of the West. She asked me to tell her what "so-called Christians" believe. (My students loved to use the expression "so-called" and employed it any chance they got, appropriately or not.) I hesitated. It was an odd thing to share the major credos of one's faith with someone observing you as dispassionately and superiorly as she might a chemical reaction or a bug. I knew she was no seeker—at least not at that moment.

I went through the basic tenets and then halted after I talked about the rising from the dead part and how the Spirit kept the church going. Long silence.

Xiao Zhang stared back at me incredulously. The sunset glinted coldly off her glasses. "You believe *that*!?"

She never was the soul of tact.

My family went to church. My mother considered overseeing our faith as her primary and most significant parenting responsibility. It was her duty to make sure we had a firm grasp of scripture and the Bible. I was baptized in Camden's stately, whitewashed Methodist church, where long rows of pansies in the side yard flanked the sidewalk between the brick education building and the sanctuary. The church employed an African American gardener, George, who did not attend church there. Even when I was only three years old, I addressed him by his first name. George would offer to let me pick the pansies. "Some flowers grow when you pick them more," he told me. It was magical to be asked to pick flowers.

After a few years of attending that nice and very respectable Methodist church, my parents transferred to the small, redbricked Lutheran church three blocks away. My mother's family was Lutheran, and my father said he could never get it out of her.

I was older when I recognized the invisible lines of social class reflected in church attendance in my town, at least for whites. (Black citizens had their own constellation of churches.) One could attend the Episcopal, Presbyterian, Methodist, Lutheran, Baptist, and Pentecostal, with Pentecostal being the bottom social rung. Catholics were removed from this equation entirely—they had their own (one) church on Fair Street.

Sundays were all about church. While my mother insisted on baths almost every night of the week, Saturday night marked our most vigorous ablutions. When my sisters and I lined up for Mom to curl our hair for church, wrapping the thin ends of our locks in toilet paper and fixing them to our heads with bobby pins, we were allowed to watch television. We each had a Sunday dress and Sunday shoes used only for church.

My mother never cooked on Sunday. It was the only day of the week that I remember her staying in the bed most of the afternoon, reading. We got a tray of food from the school's mess hall and ate leftovers for supper. Sometimes on Sunday nights she would lead us in small lessons on the Bible.

Soon I read the Bible on my own. Furtively, under the light of my bedroom closet, I began with Genesis and read straight through the endless levitical codes and the narratives of Judges and Kings, the Psalms, and the New Testament. I took it all seriously. Because my life experience was relatively free of care, I found it easy to believe in a God who looked out for me. Each morning at school, I recited the Pledge of Allegiance, its cadences echoing from the wooden speaker mounted above the chalkboard. I had been taught that the United States was the greatest, most free country in the world and that it treated people equally. Despite unsettling and surreal racial disparities, I did not yet question either of those assertions. The system worked for my family.

I spent a lot of time alone in my growing up years. For the most part, this did not bother me. I loved to walk out into the long-leaf pine forest, sidle up a tree to one of the many platforms my sisters and I had built, and sit, reading or watching the deep emerald of the long needles glimmer and shift with light. I loved the whispers of the wind. I loved the resonant, heady smell of pine. I would drop everything to go watch the sun dip into the horizon. I spent a lot of time talking quietly to God in the scrub oaks.

They were not one-way conversations. I had some powerful experiences of God's presence. Once, sitting alone in my small Lutheran church, the afternoon light on the cross grew brilliant and mesmerizing. I sat three-quarters of the way back in the sanctuary's plain, wooden pews, praying. I often slipped into the sanctuary in silence to do this. No sound, no air stirred. But I felt a glowing and palpable sense not only of God's presence but also of Jesus' sacrifice—what it might have meant to pour himself over the wounds of the world. I felt an almost tangible sense of salvation—redemption—envelop me. I have no idea how long I sat there, as occasional cars drove by on the side street and the cries of children climbing the gnarled oak tree in the yard floated through the wooden doors. There was a powerful force in that room, and it knew my name.

Several months later my church community was electrified—and divided—by hosting a Lay Witness program. This was a lay group who came for a week of evening services. They brought with them an informal worship style and a message of personal conversion different from the orderly and comforting Lutheran liturgy with its haunting, sung responses and careful repetitions and pauses. I loved liturgy. The old-fashioned, elegant language and medieval minor harmonies preserved in the battered, red hymnals were comforting precisely because of the tradition behind them. The repetition did not bore me but rather allowed the words to press themselves inside me until they were instinctive. The rising and falling cadences seemed to hold my prayer.

Some of the adults were unsettled by the visitors with their contemporary worship style and focus on the Holy Spirit. It was my first introduction to the clashes and conflicts that faithful Christians have over theology and the validity of certain religious experiences. The conflict was very different from the moments of intimacy I felt with God in my quiet forest sanctuary where questions of credibility, theological division, and religious correctness (a minefield upon which I would spend so much wasted time later) never even surfaced.

Though I did not grasp what was going on, my church had encountered a new spiritual movement. Call it "Pentecostal," "charismatic," "Spirit-filled," "evangelical," or "free church," this movement stirred segments of many traditional, mainline Protestant churches in the South and beyond. And its mystical and powerful manifestations of spiritual presence sowed controversy everywhere.

My mother began reading the Bible more devotedly and poring over paperbacks in which people told dramatic stories of healings and changing lives by bringing people to Jesus. She began to listen to recordings of sermons, and she went to hear speakers at other churches. My dad did not share or understand her born-again enthusiasm and largely steered clear. When the small subset of congregational members who were deeply affected by the week of the Lay Witness program began meeting in one another's homes, my mother joined them. Sometimes they met at our house.

I would sit at the top of the stairwell and listen to the sounds of worship float up. Someone would read scripture, and I heard a sudden shift into unintelligible phrases surrounded by the soft murmurings of others or exclamations. This, I knew, was speaking in tongues. New phrases entered in my spiritual lexicon—"born again," "having a heart" for something, "turning your life over to Jesus," the "four spiritual laws," and the preeminent "personal relationship with Jesus Christ." I heard these phrases alongside the other more familiar ones: "Lamb of God, who takes away the sin of the world," "things done and left undone," "we have not loved you with our whole heart."

I was a reconciler. The particular insight—that we were all carrying partial truth and actually needed one another to arrive at any understanding that was whole—was instinctive to me. But finding where I fit in was a bit harder. While the charismatic movement claimed to care only about believers having vital, Spirit-infused faiths, its litmus tests revolved around its own trinity: the manifestation of spiritual gifts of healing, prophecy, and speaking in tongues.

I was not gifted. I had no evidence that my prayers miraculously and instantaneously healed people. No gracefully worded prophetic utterances, spoken in the syntax of Isaiah, rolled off my tongue. I remember spending an entire evening at the top of the stairs, muttering gibberish and wondering, somehow, if I were actually speaking in tongues.

The lack of a discernible gift of the Spirit deeply troubled me. Until that point, I had been content and joyful in the organic and simple faith of my childhood. But now it did not seem to be enough. Insider status within the charismatic movement could not be achieved merely by pious or good behavior. There were tests to pass. No matter how fervent my prayer as I traveled the woods and pastures, no matter how certain I was of God's blessing, no matter how the loveliness of the world called out songs of praise from me, I felt my lack acutely. I had not passed those tests. That reality left open the question of where the Holy Spirit was in my life and what exactly was the status of my personal relationship with Jesus Christ.

Now, of course, I have a different understanding. I know that the language of faith is no meritocracy, nor is there any single path toward God. Paul's teaching on the gifts of the Spirit is intended to point us toward the variety and diversity of spiritual gifts, not to the supremacy of three. But when I was young and shaping my identity in the world, my distorted understanding told me that I had to have the right kind of faith. There were acceptable proofs and unacceptable proofs. The church—even that evangelical contingent focused on renewing the church—did what it always seemed to do and sorted itself by those who were "in" and those who were "out."

Faith holds that space between the mystery of God and our own proffered hand, an intimate relationship essentially known and understood by the two parties involved. But incarnated in our deeply flawed human community, it is never merely this. We must use the right phrases, express proper political viewpoints, care about certain political issues, and ignore other political ramifications. We must fit in, adopting whatever perspectives currently bears the biblical stamp of approval, and these vary by community. Every community has a code, and lip service to that code determines our acceptance and inclusion.

Despite the questions that the Lay Witness experience unleashed in me, its brand of evangelicalism also gave me some life-changing gifts. I became more expectant in my faith and more adept at mining the beautiful wisdom of scripture and the word of God. It was a spirituality that expected and looked for the renewing presence of God every day. It gave me the courage to be odd and noncomformist in a world running amok.

Ultimately, this strand of my spiritual heritage helped me become a person who was both stronger and more grounded. I emerged from my childhood unconcerned about the status quo and not entirely trusting of all forms of spiritual leadership. I did not care for cultural norms or spiritual orthodoxy. And I knew that whatever we were given our lives for, it had little to do with making a living and was a lot more important than money. These were all good qualities with which to enter adulthood.

I look back at Xiao Zhang and think of the spirituality of my childhood. I could not express my entire spiritual path to her. The vital sense of a creative, loving, powerful presence on this earth came to me as a child, whispering through many things—nature, the church, my parents, and that Lay Witness mission that swung open the door and let the Spirit blast in. It came through intense and unexpected revelations that were almost mystical. These revelations could not be summoned but came through the veil like invitations.

We can be taught about God, but ultimately we must seek the experience of God. And God and Jesus must come and get us. For the most part, the institutional church has been less than helpful in that process. It has tried to scare us into God's pen, pull us into that pen, and tell us the pen is made of boards of respectability. It has tried to tell us that it matters what flock we are in and then divides us up by breed and color. It has done everything except lead us to the edge of the woods at sunset and ask us to breathe.

And when it has scared, pulled, beaten, or built that pen around us, the church has asked for our full attention. It wants to teach us our mission in life, mostly driving home the lesson that the only reason any believer exists is to go out and get more animals in the pen. But the function of faith is fundamentally different. Faith beckons us to the edge of that forest—its sun-splattered glades, its lovely, looming shadows and uncertain paths—unbinds us, and urges us to wander toward the sun.

PART II

Threshold and Door

Now there came a day when Elisha passed over to Shunem, where there was a prominent woman, and she persuaded him to eat food. And so it was, as often as he passed by, he turned in there to eat food. She said to her husband, "Behold now, I perceive that this is a holy man of God passing by us continually. Please, let us make a little walled upper chamber and let us set a bed for him there, and a table and a chair and a lampstand; and it shall be, when he comes to us, that he can turn in there." One day he came there and turned in to the upper chamber and rested.

2 Kings 4:8-11

Build a room; a window against the sky.

Welcome what comes.

Light, darkness, wind, storm.

The voices of strangers

will teach you.

Chapter 5

A Room for the Wayfarer

The story begins with an open door. Someone leaves home to travel. Someone else welcomes the wanderer, shares food, table, and space. We need the wanderer. We need that open door of welcome.

Those who have come before us leave us spiritual disciplines as clues for finding our way in this world. One of these disciplines is pilgrimage. Another is journey. The two differ. Pilgrimage is built around the end result; one launches with an eye on a destination. Journey involves wandering, looking for God on the path, and being unsure where the path will end.

Abram, Lot, Sarai, Lot's wife—God asks them to leave their home with no sense of destination. The journey stretches before them for a lifetime. Under the leadership of Moses, the people of God wander the desert forty years, a reality echoed in Jesus' own forty-day wandering through the wilderness after his baptism and before beginning his ministry. The wandering brings us into the land of promise or vocation—into our lives.

Jesus follows in the tradition of many holy men—including Elisha, the one who visited Shunem—because he is itinerant. He travels the regions of Galilee and Jerusalem with no set place to call home, relying on hospitality—the welcome and shelter of strangers. Yet hospitality hinges also on the capacity of those strangers to attend to and notice him. To welcome the holy man, one must first see him and recognize his need.

A few stunning and powerful ideas in the story of the Shunammite woman parallel the learnings of my own life. First is that hospitality—the simple act of opening a door to the stranger—is beautifully dangerous. Equally lovely and revolutionary is the experience of being hosted. These are the most revolutionary gestures that we make to one another. They have the power to reshape our entire lives.

In the story of the Shunammite woman in Second Kings, hospitality grows like a powerful vine. She first simply notices the holy man who passes through her town on the way to somewhere else. Her first gesture is to feed him. From such humble seeds, the idea of a holy room grows. The woman builds a place for prayer, for rest, for encounter with the Holy. The shared hospitality grows into something more permanent: a grounded relationship.

Only when we practice a hospitality that welcomes people while making it clear that we need something they offer us in return can transformation at the deepest level occur. When we live by the conviction that everyone brings a gift that someone else desperately needs, we move from hospitality to relationship. There is always a place for hospitality, but over time the Divine yearns for us to move into relationship. And if we continually insist on being the host—the dispenser of hospitality—we essentially cling to privilege and ignore the gifts of others.

My friend Scott recently sent me a letter in which he wrestles with relationship, hospitality, and privilege. He wrote the following:

> I think about that story of the rich young man. In global typography, he is I. Jesus' call is not to give all we have to become destitute, hopeless, a person without options. The invitation is to follow Jesus, which I think has something to do with letting go of the false sense of security that people associate with wealth. It is an invitation to live in the moment, with

whoever is before you, to receive with gratitude the hospitality of others.

This is one of the edges in my spiritual life. I can go without and live simply far more easily than I can accept hospitality from someone I judge not to have enough for themselves.

When I went to help after hurricane Katrina, I drove along the coast of Louisiana. Every telephone and electric pole was snapped like a toothpick. Houses were ripped open like tin cans. I found myself staring at the backside of people's closets. As the afternoon drew to a close, I stopped at a local emergency management headquarters. After a brief visit, the man in charge asked me to stay for dinner. I remonstrated, explaining I had a car and knew where I could get food back in Baton Rouge. I knew their food was scarce. He grew a bit angry and said we were acting like FEMA folks, passing through quickly without receiving what the people had to offer. That did it! I enjoyed the finest catfish dinner that I've ever had. To think that another cannot afford to give you anything—or worse, to believe he or she has nothing you might need—is such a vestige of privilege. It becomes a deep barrier to love.

I consider my own story, the hospitality others offered me, the ways that they opened their lives. Hospitality has allowed me to break down divisions, barriers, and misperceptions. Any border-crossing I have done has been possible because of hospitality. Ultimately, people have welcomed me deeply and invited me to make myself at home with them. More than anything else, this extension of some intimacy, some trust with their lives, is precisely what allowed me to begin to see the world in a different way. People have taken me in—shared their houses, their food, their families—and shaken apart all my assumptions. I have taken people into my home, which sparked an internal journey into knowing myself better. The hospitality of others is the most transformative force I know. It made me wish to live in a way that was worthy of their generosity. Hospitality taught me to love better.

The practice of hospitality is the only authentic antidote to the cultural propensity to operate in increasingly stratified realities. We live in a world defined by schism and full of political litmus tests. Hospitality dismantles balkanization and reduction, ideological polarization, and black-and-white thinking. It makes us human to one another. And when it does that, it also breaks down our barriers. Never underestimate the ability of hospitality to engender true, transformative revolution. It will come as a revolution with a human face, devoid of ideology and political partisanship.

Hospitality forces us to take in the real and complex person at our door—the person right in front of us who may be different than we are—as opposed to seeking out only certain people. Our technological age gives us tremendous capacity to remain insular, and it can also increase and reinforce that insularity. Whatever my beliefs, the web of technology allows me to find those who support my viewpoints. Without those who can challenge our thinking, we may sink deeper and deeper into our own perspectives. I can create a virtual community of assent instead of living in a real, incarnated community of characters, conflict, and compromises. We often use the Internet to reinforce our own paradigms. It is no wonder that we find our country (and world) convulsed in unprecedented political polarization.

Back in Shunem, one woman's choice to show hospitality and one man's decision to accept it slowly turn their lives upside down. Quietly and unobtrusively, hospitality morphs into a path of holiness. The prophet might need more—a place to rest and pray and study. The offering of a meal becomes a plan to build an entire room. And the room becomes an invitation for her to spend time there in Elisha's absence. It becomes a place for her.

Hospitality—whether we accept it or offer it—can steer our lives off the beaten, predictable path. And when it veers off in a new direction, gifts come—unexpected and even miraculous gifts.

Chapter 6

Crossing the Border

I had to leave home to begin to understand who my people were. I was twenty when I first crossed the border.

After high school, I attended Duke University on a scholarship package that allowed me to study abroad during my junior year. In many ways, college life itself already felt like living in a foreign country compared to my small hometown in South Carolina. When I left the United States for France after two years on Duke's campus, my travels just continued the disorientation and culture shock I had experienced since my first semester of college.

When I arrived on Duke's campus that first day in my carefully selected freshman attire, I was flagrantly ignorant of the dominant preppy culture. I wore bright yellow, capri-length overalls over a striped T-shirt. My wedge espadrilles were rainbow-colored, tied up to midcalf with ballet strap fastenings. My parents unloaded my new, faux-leather suitcases (a graduation present), placed my clothes in my closet (not a polo shirt or a pair of khakis among them), put the patterned sheets on the twin bed in my half of the room, helped me hang the cool art prints I had bought at Roses department store, arranged my incidentals (a few books, a green dictionary and thesaurus, some pictures) on the small brown desk, and left.

All the ways that I had prepared myself for school seemed insubstantial. My carefully chosen clothes were out of step. (I wasn't exactly a clotheshorse, but I fancied myself as having a bit of style, and my mother—a skilled seamstress—teamed with me in design. Mom and I had moved from Simplicity to Vogue patterns, from polyester to 100-percent cotton, wool, and silk. These were undeniable class moves up.)

I was taken aback by the definitive mind-set that other students brought to their schooling. They were premed, prelaw, or public policy. Everyone assumed that he or she would attend graduate school. I came with a whole set of naïve and, yes, scholarly goals. My parents had passed down a strong belief in the "liberal arts education," which I thought meant "learning for learning's sake." My parents wanted their children to be educated, but that education was never linked to a specific profession, and I don't remember a conversation in which I was encouraged to pursue a field of study because of the job behind it. (Perhaps this was because we were all women, and it was not assumed that we would be primary supporters of our families.) Ultimately, this gave me the permission to make the choices that shaped my life.

My first week at Duke, I ran into the only other person I knew from my hometown. "How's it going?" she asked.

I could barely keep the tears from welling up as I struggled to tame the tremor in my voice. "I'm going to flunk out," I told her.

"But it's only your first week!" she responded, clearly puzzled.

My fear of flunking out pushed me to study hard; I took classes, memorized facts, and forgot them. I was a good girl. I made my first forays into the dog-eat-dog world of creative writing, where I listened to classmates read, then watched their compatriots circle around for the kill, each trying to make the more insightful critical comment to "improve" the piece. I felt flush with pride when an internationally acclaimed professor-novelist admitted me into his course based on my writing samples—and then I hastily dropped it after the first class because I thought I'd never been in the presence of a more arrogant teacher whose primary goal was to intimidate students.

We only begin to know ourselves by crossing borders. We learn who we are by becoming other, by being a stranger. I first learned this by attending Duke, but it was a lesson I continued to learn over the course of my college career. If I loved my region and my family for giving me a strong sense of identity, I came to recognize that identity most fully by leaving home.

My decision to study in France my junior year of college was pivotal. In France, I endured my most sustained experience with vulnerability, that wonderful tutor of our adult years, by trying to live immersed in the language. When we begin to speak a language at the conversational level, we often feel like children. People treat us like infants. We think like adults but express ourselves like two-year-olds.

My cross-cultural rules were straightforward: Avoid compatriots and other English speakers. Avoid speaking my own language. Find groups in the host culture and participate in them as much as my outsider status allows. Avoid bashing the host culture and be generous to my own. Avoid groups of foreigners who like to engage in such bashing. Speak the new language as much as possible. Because I couldn't speak the new language conversationally and avoided speaking my own, I found myself doing a lot of listening and cultural observation. This was not a bad thing.

Later, after spending more time in other cultures, I added another rule: Whatever I think I understand about a culture or group after spending extensive time there, ditch it. Whatever grasp I think I have on the culture after one year, I should be prepared to totally turn it on its head in the second year.

I studied in Aix-en-Provence, host of many language institutes. French instructors taught my classes in the French language inside a small building on a quiet side street. The program taught grammar and a smattering of literature, history, and art in an integrated way. As my fellow students and I studied impressionism, we read the literature and studied the political, social, and economic histories of the same era. Why hadn't my entire school life done this? I was enthralled.

I joined a choir, composed of French students who sang in English, at the local university. (This didn't break my rule since I used the activity to meet other French students.) I found a small church to attend on Sundays. It was connected to a Christian community on the outskirts of town that I visited regularly. I took a ceramics class, where I met a friendly French woman who introduced me to her daughter Beatrice. Once Beatrice talked me into hitchhiking into the country. A gardener in a small, red pickup gave us a ride, and we spent the day in beautiful fields of wild poppies and watching old men play *peton,* the traditional game of painted wooden balls, in the brilliant sun.

I met Nichole and Lionel, a Vietnamese and French couple, on the street, and we spent long evenings in their tiny loft apartment discussing culture, history, and how to make *salade nicoise,* the staple of our diet those nights. They were probably radical communists, if I could have understood their vocabulary.

I was especially intrigued by my history teacher, who wore the same shabby, gray, loose-fitting sweater all semester. His long, shaggy hair swung unkempt around his pale face. Rectangular, black-rimmed glasses masked only slightly the intensity of his eyes. He had nicotine-yellow teeth and smoked like a chimney. When he lectured, he paced restlessly across the front of the classroom, gesticulating fiercely to make a point, never slowing down his barrage of French to bring us up to speed. I had the impression that he resented us slightly, possibly because we were all so young, so very naïve and sheltered, and so confidently ignorant. But I thought that I had not ever met someone who was so thoughtful and brilliant and dedicated to study.

My watershed moment occurred one day when he strode into the classroom, slammed the door behind him, perched himself on the desk, and glared at the back of the room. "Do you realize that early this morning, US President Jimmy Carter launched a military operation into Iran to rescue the hostages?"

My fellow students and I did not know. We were not the most politically informed group. Most of us possessed a vague awareness of the Iranian revolution, which had started in the middle of my freshman year and climaxed with Khomeini's installation in power several months previous. We had heard of the fifty-two Americans taken hostage the previous November.

My first inclination was to celebrate. The rescue, though perhaps stupidly risky, seemed valiant. (As it happened, it failed, star-crossed by sandstorms.) But I looked at the teacher's visibly disturbed face and waited.

"Do you understand the implication? Iran is in crisis! Any action like this on the part of your country could destabilize the entire world. This kind of unilateral military action is irresponsible!" He launched himself off the desk and paced the front of the room like an angry tiger.

My father would hate this guy, I thought. But the lesson stuck. I realized that I was used to thinking of US politics as just that—US politics. I was accustomed to thinking of the country as an entity. Maybe the United States didn't do a very good job of teaching other languages, maybe we didn't have a strong awareness of other cultures, maybe we didn't think that what we decided to do was anyone else's business, but we were the original Lone Rangers, right? I suddenly pondered responsibility and accountability within a larger global community. My feelings were vague and conflicted as I struggled to negotiate this new information. I knew that my teacher with the crazy hair who was hunched over his desk was giving me something I would not find in my own culture. I appreciated the dissonance. Instinctively I realized he had made a solid point, one that the frenzied media coverage in the United States would not be making. The message came through to me only because I happened to be sitting outside the border at the time.

Border-crossing can offer many gifts. I encountered questions I would never have asked. I began to see myself and my homeland in a different, often unflattering, light. I released at last the quiet certainty that can lead to blindness as easily as it can lead to truth. Taken altogether, my first experience in crossing borders was fairly humbling and sometimes humiliating, both constructive spiritual processes.

Suddenly, my stint in France was over, and I found myself back at Duke for my senior year. I worried about what in the heck I was going to do after college. I often walked the quiet, off-campus neighborhood streets and peered furtively into the brightly lit windows. Inside were messy sofas, jumbled coffee tables, and families eating around tables. Those ordinary scenes unleashed and ache and sense of longing that overpowered me. I felt more than homesickness. I sensed a primal longing for a home that seemed impossibly far away.

Many of my classmates had their plans in place, and for most of them, the future involved graduate school—lots of medicine and law, business and public policy. People like me who had majored in English and history because they loved to read books and write papers decided they might like to dodge graduate school and interview for jobs in the "Real World." I interviewed with a furniture company in High Point, North Carolina, about the possibility of writing marketing copy. I interviewed with an insurance company about being an underwriter (surely it would *have* to deal with writing, yes?). I passed on the bank interviews. I stared out the window a lot. *There must be better work out there,* I thought.

In the end, I declined all my job offers. Midyear, at the urging of my campus minister, I'd talked to a representative of the Lutheran Volunteer Corps about the urban volunteer program, a year of service in a ministry focused on different areas of social service and policy. Volunteers—others who also had no idea what to do and probably majored in English and history or maybe religion, which was worse—lived together in community. They received room, board, health insurance, and $35 monthly discretionary spending money. I signed on and was placed in Washington, D.C. Before I knew it, commencement weekend arrived. I had not flunked out.

A year of working with people who needed basics like food and clothing or helping elders or children make their way in the world. while in a house with other people where we might have a messy living room and eat supper together, sure sounded better than writing copy about furniture in an apartment in High Point. I'd seen my parents do work they cared about. I'd seen them give almost everything they had to build the school that they believed in. Like them, I wanted to find my way to good work. I wanted work that possessed the potential to heal someone—me, someone else, I wasn't picky.

For the next decade, I would largely learn by being a voyeur, living in very different communities. I would spend the summer immersed in a rural, African American community in North Carolina. I would spend two years in D.C.'s inner city. I lived almost two years in China. Three decades later would find me still living and working in some of the poorest neighborhoods of urban Philadelphia. I was searching for a way to live in this world, and I still am.

The Lutheran Volunteer Corps program started in late August of the year I graduated from college. Three months of summer lay before me. I'd taken a two-month summer job with an organization focused on rural health issues in North Carolina. Grad school was about to begin.

Chapter 7

To Dream a World Beyond Race

After graduation, I found myself reading the words of a guy named Saul Alinsky. I had signed on as a community organizer with the North Carolina Student Rural Health Coalition, a nonprofit out of Chapel Hill and Duke medical schools that provided very basic care to underserved populations in rural North Carolina. My job was to work in the host community that they had chosen as a site that summer, helping to set up a two-week health clinic and following up with the community afterward.

Alinsky wrote the primer on the principles of community organizing that was supposed to help me do this job. I wasn't sure how to apply Alinsky's urban examples to Como, a rural crossroads in eastern North Carolina with four buildings—a filling station, a church, a post office, and a fertilizer shed. Fewer than one hundred people lived within the town limits, which encompassed about three square miles. Most of the inhabitants were white—surprising because the county was actually 65 percent African American (and then, not surprising at all).

The community was familiar in a haunting way. I recognized the long workdays; the large farm equipment; the tiny, beleaguered community clinging to the small collegial structures that held it together— church, gas station, post office, volunteer fire department. The land, like that of the South Carolina low country, was rich and flat with dark, lazy rivers. Farmers grew soybeans, corn, and cotton—just like my uncles and cousins—as well as peanuts and tobacco. The farms that remained were big operations owned by whites. Like the South Carolina low country, this part of North Carolina had once been a plantation stronghold, so its racial demographics were similar. But if I thought my own South Carolina roots would make me seem less of an outsider and agitator, I was dead wrong.

Our team did not have an auspicious launch of the summer health program. The two black churches in the area that were sponsoring the health fair and housing its workers hadn't imagined it was necessary to get approval from county commissioners to run a two-week health fair in the smallest incorporated crossroad in the county. The county commissioners disagreed. Before I arrived, a sheriff came through the black neighborhoods searching "for white students living in homes."

This region had always been uneasy about race. Nat Turner's rebellion took place a stone's throw up the road in neighboring Southampton County, Virginia, a hundred and fifty years before. The most devastating outcome of Turner's uprising might have been the edict forbidding any white person to teach a black person in the South to read.

Almost all of my days and nights were spent in Como's African American community. Those in the community housed me, fed me, told me their stories, took me to their churches and into their families, let me work in their gardens, and taught me to pick chicken feathers. They offered me an almost unimaginable gift—the hospitality of sharing homes and families across the polite and inviolate lines of black and white. It broke the rule that defined all racial interaction in the South: Be as tight as you want in the day, but be in your own neighborhood come nightfall.

I stayed with about seven families over the summer, one white. In the African American homes, I learned about hair—braiding it, greasing it, using straightening combs. I learned about cooking—when I asked for recipes, I was perpetually flummoxed. "Oh, you know, add a little flour and a little milk and sugar," I was told. "Add some eggs if you have them." When I asked how long something should cook, I was told, "Till it's about right." I might have cooked sauces using such seat-of-the-pants methods but never an entire three-layer cake! It was a summer of learning language, cadence, expression, stories, and interpersonal communication. It was about seeing what was held as valuable and precious by the different groups, seeing how community was built, and seeing what was treasured.

I spent my days visiting. My job was to tell every household in the community about the health fair and try to get people involved in organizing it. Nights brought more community visits or hanging out—watching TV, visiting the neighbors, or making friends. We'd listen to preachers on the radio or just talk on the back porch. I listened to lots of stories in such colorful language that I enjoyed. But I heard tragedies too, like ancient Ms. Martie Green telling me about the death of her veteran husband. I asked her if she would attend the health fair, and she asked me if I knew about the Tuskegee Institute study for syphilis. (I knew nothing of this forty-year study in which the US Public Health service studied the national progression of untreated syphilis in six hundred poor, black sharecroppers. The men were not told they had syphilis and were not treated, even though an effective cure existed.) Ms. Martie gave me my first education in the historically justified suspicion some black Americans brought to the healthcare system.

Gradually, I noticed how the world assumed whiteness as the norm. Whiteness was the monolithic, soundless backdrop to everything. The phone book cover pictured a small, blond girl in a pink dress talking on the telephone. Television shows seemed ubiquitously white. White people whose personal dilemmas, set in affluent homes with manicured decors, dominated soap operas. The evening news, anchored by white faces, was predisposed to stories dominated by crime and mug shots of dark-skinned men. The ads in the paper sported white faces; pictures of Jesus on the weekly church bulletins were white. Nowhere I looked did I see the world in which I now lived.

The African American men of Como worked like Trojans. Most of the men in their thirties and forties no longer worked on farms.

Instead, they had jobs in factories, machine plants, or at the shipyard three hours away. The homes of the older farm workers were shabbier and visibly run-down, set in the country away from the modern neighborhoods of brick ranch homes.

I heard stories from the women who worked in the homes of the white families in town. "I took care of old Ms. Barrett till the day she died—fed her, washed her like a baby, changed her soiled sheets. And when I showed up at the funeral, Old Mr. Barrett told me to sit at the back of the church. I just walked out of that church and never went back. By then Willie had a job at the slaughterhouse. I didn't need that job." When I complimented Sara Brown's hydrangea, brilliant blue against the weather-beaten gray of her unpainted home, she responded, "Oh, that comes from a clipping I got off Mrs. Smith's tree in her yard. Raised it right up myself. But do you know she begrudged me that? She was always a covetous woman." Some of the women were still in touch with the families they had worked for. The black folk of the community knew the white folk by name; the white folk didn't seem to know the names of the black folk. It was a familiar dynamic.

I roamed among all the families, the stories, the parcels of land and river, gathering lore like so many herbs and charms. I wandered cemeteries, white and black. The family names were the same. Reared on the complex lineage of Southern families, I loved to unravel the intricate web of relationships in that community.

In a farming community, land carries a great deal of weight. I could tell almost everything about social relationships in the community by land allocation. The low lots, the poorer lots along the highway, the parcels well outside of town were developed into "black neighborhoods." These unincorporated areas were among the most densely populated in the county. Despite this, traffic could and did barrel through them at highway speeds. Lower speed limit postings were reserved for the (white) houses in city limits, though most of those houses had much larger yard frontage and were removed from the highway.

There were few black farmers in the county, and their acreage was tiny compared to the large tracts of the white farmers. One of the families I lived with had lost its farm in the past ten years. The stories they told about their childhood on the farm had a haunting sense of finality and loss.

One night after supper, a friend and I dropped by her mother's house, a little white clapboard in need of paint, set off by itself. We stood on a fence rail looking out over a field. "That was my daddy's farm," she said quietly. "I can still see him driving that tractor around. He loved that tractor—worked years to buy it. We had to sell all of it—the land, the equipment, that old shed." She looked to the right at an unpainted shed and then back at the field. "I did everything on this farm to help my father growing up—milked, planted, kept the chickens and the garden. But all the small farmers, which here means all the black farmers—they got pushed out. I guess he never got over it. He died two years afterward." She looked at me. "How long do you think he could stay alive, living next to his lost land like that?"

I looked across the flat, rich fields that edged into swamp, pondering our interwoven ancestry. Her ancestors were captured; the few who survived the middle passage were brought to work this land. Through the pressure of many white people of conscience, and a war, they were liberated—into nothing. No forty acres and no mule, just Jim Crow law, a sharecropper system, and a region eviscerated by war and social chaos. It took decades for them to have a small piece of land, and that space opened for only a short time.

I thought how my ancestors—French Huguenot, Swiss-German, and German—came to the United States with little property but of their own volition. Some fled intense persecution. A few may have been indentured servants, working alongside slaves and at other hard-labor craft jobs for a decade before being released as free agents. The Southern economy in these flat, coastal regions was erected on oppression and exploitation. How I wish my relatives had been among the voices of visionary, transformative dissent—the abolitionists, the stops on the Underground Railroad, the quiet resisters.

I wanted to be a person like that in the world; I wanted to be from people like that. But no stories of heroic dissent have come down to me, so I can only assume they all kept the status quo.

Mr. Timmy Branch came over to Ms. Margaret's house every night for a supper plate. He was a bachelor and never cooked. He'd seat himself on the outside steps or in the chair at the side of the kitchen. (Ms. Margaret never allowed his work clothes and boots any farther.) Sometimes he didn't say a word, and sometimes he had a lot on his mind. He kept pigs, chickens, and a garden, and he watched over the neighborhood's comings and goings. Every time he got my attention, he'd fix his eyes, with their pale yellow orbs and copper lighted irises on my gray-green ones: "You be particular going up and down that road, Miss Dee. Watch yourself out there."

Mr. Branch's words spoke to me of the coping strategy of an old black man who knew the world to be full of powers that could control you, harm you, and alter your life. There in that little cluster of houses and lots, he had his livelihood, modest as it was, and he had neighbors he knew. He believed in staying home, out of folks' way, not attracting attention, and not dealing with anyone unless he had to. He followed a particular set of rules in his life—he was careful about where he went, who he talked to, what he said, and what he let on understanding. He knew that the world could do him fundamental harm. His was the wisdom adopted by people living under duress.

The world being dominated by pale-skinned folks, me being one of them, I did not need this wisdom as much. Survival was on my side in a big way. But I was old enough to honor where his advice came from. I knew it was neither provincial nor ill-placed.

That easy summer, with its heat and long days, earth spilling with flowers, vegetables, and fruits, sun beckoning in the morning and moon filtering into backyards at night, extended its hand and promised me a dream. That summer, I lived as though race was not a rock on which our country had broken itself again and again. It was so easy to let that hospitable, caring, and relational community take me in that I forgot to think about race.

For me, that summer was the moment I experienced the cool draught of grace. I was taken in and cared for in a way that I was surprised any Black community would do for a naïve, white girl. In return, I tried to pay attention and learn my racial lessons. This was the unexpected miracle God brought to birth in my life—a chance to imagine a world beyond the strictures of race. Silences around race had punctuated my entire life. Here, finally, was a new possibility built on authentic relationships rather than political or social conviction. It was thrilling to consider the prospect of genuine knowing across the chasm of cultural unknowing I'd received as part of my racial inheritance. I welcomed the cracking of the great monolith of white culture.

Little did I know then that such a summer would never come again. At moments in my life I would again experience deep racial reconciliation and relationship but never quite as fully as that summer. Never again have I experienced the demon of racial prejudice so powerfully redeemed in my daily interactions. Como and the community found and created there altered my life choices in fundamental ways. It made me leave the white track I probably would have followed, where my life was primarily lived around the company of other white people. From that time, I've chosen my schools, my faith communities, and my circles differently. Never again have I lived in a predominantly white neighborhood. I choose workplaces that focus on justice, where conversation about how race impacts us all is standard. I've tried to learn my racial lessons, spending decades peeling back the layers of what it means to be white in America's culture and what that privilege injects into my daily assumptions and interactions.

All this because of the dream that I glimpsed—the possibility of a land where race finally and utterly loses its power. That dream became part of me. It has never come true, and it has never let me go.

Chapter 8

Life in the Red-Light District

When I pointed my little Chevy toward D.C. at the end of August for a year with the Lutheran Volunteer Corps, I felt like I had lost home twice. Behind me in South Carolina lay the region that had given me my whole identity. Behind me in North Carolina was a little town that had shown me who I was in a new and redemptive way. Ahead lay the city, an environment in which I had never lived nor imagined living.

My community house stood at the center of D.C.'s red-light district. My placement for the year, located about three doors away, was at Bread for the City, then a tiny, walk-in center that handed out emergency food bags and free clothes to folks who stopped by. They also tried to do some low-level social work, connecting these folks to services that were a bit more substantial than T-shirts and peanut butter or tuna.

Later, many of us who worked in the cities, whose centers were magnets for those most disenfranchised by the economic system, would realize that the early 1980s saw the birth of homelessness as a social issue. The sixties had given rise to the promising vision of mental health deinstitutionalization, where the mental-health system would be transformed by moving away from human warehouses to community-based centers with case management and support services. But that dream was never realized because funding for the transition was diverted, and refugees from the emptied mental hospitals fell through the cracks without adequate new systems in place. During the Reagan administration, federal housing supports for low-income housing were cut drastically. It was a perfect storm.

We should not have been surprised when thousands of mentally ill and marginalized people ended up on the streets in cities throughout the United States. First, news stories talked of "homeless people." Slowly, however, the adjective shifted to a noun. Suddenly, we had "the homeless" among us, and they were intractable.

A few years ago, my friend Steve, a brilliant math teacher and astute social observer, was teaching his students the principle of correlated graphs. To show how graphs can illustrate the relationships between two sets of statistics, he first graphed the cuts in federal housing subsidies from late 1979 to 1984, and then, as an overlay, graphed the corresponding rise in the population of persons who were homeless during the same five-year period. The two graphs inversely mirrored each other. He looked out at a swarm of baffled faces. It took a while for him to realize that the students were not thinking about his graphs at all. Rather, they were stunned by the realization that there had even been a time in US history when there had been almost no persons without homes.

Homeless individuals were among the fixtures of my days in the Lutheran Volunteer Corps. They lived on the steps of my home or came into Bread for the City every day. We all need our routine, and people who live with no permanent shelter are no different.

People become homeless for many reasons. Not all of those reasons fit into our pat political paradigms, but our political schemata reflect the reasons we choose to embrace and the ones we ignore. The political views applied to the lives I saw around me were endless and in direct conflict. Some people targeted dependencies caused by well-intentioned but disempowering social safety nets. Others pointed to the devastation of our urban neighborhoods, their economic structures gutted and their schools abandoned. Many pointed fingers at racism and classism, while others pleaded for individuals to take more personal responsibility. Other voices implored that these lives be touched by the power of God and redeemed in one fell swoop by the Spirit. There were no simple answers.

I stayed in D.C. for two years. In the life of an urban neighborhood, two years is nothing. The people who live there are used to people like me (young, white kids who come to do something) moving along. We are transients; migrant urban-experience seekers. Our work is often a stop on the way to grad school where we can become professionals who study or work with the poor and take home nice, middle-class salaries. My prayer now, looking back, is that I did not do too much damage. Yet, for some of those itinerants, myself included, something intangible and not measurable occurred. We stayed or soon returned to those urban neighborhoods; we lived altered lives.

I collected a lot of stories around my neighborhood. One of the people who came into Bread for the City was Tim, a handsome youth from Georgia with piercing blue eyes, hands that looked fine and chiseled, and sun-touched brown hair that was matted and unkempt. He was withdrawn and distrustful. The director of Bread for the City contacted Tim's parents, and occasionally long, tortured, and grieving missives arrived from Georgia with money in them to dole out to Tim in twenty-dollar bills. Tim never acted addicted; and he didn't blow his money on drink or anything else. His arms had no needle tracks. He just seemed incredibly paranoid and withdrawn. He wouldn't look at me as he took whatever I had set aside—pants his size, a pair of warm boots, a sandwich. I thought a lot about his parents.

There was Patricia, who spent her days parked on the steps of the brownstone next door, a night shelter for homeless women. She was loquacious, funny, the block commentator. She loved to feed birds.

I met persons with brilliant minds, like Julian. Julian could read five languages and spoke fluent English, French, and Spanish. He selected the clothes with elegant cuts and kept himself as immaculate as he could while living in the shelter system. He would hand me twenty-page letters, in French or English—ruminations about life, solutions to the plight of the cities, ideological screeds. This education must have been hard-won for a brown-skinned man.

Many of the most disturbed men were Vietnam veterans. War must drive people crazy. People who joined the military wanting to serve their country should not be growing old on the streets.

There was Janice, the immaculately groomed prostitute. Janice looked to be about forty-five. She dressed professionally, and she got dropped off on the corner at 9:00 a.m. by a man whom she called her husband. He picked her up at 5:00 p.m. every day in his late-model car. She said she lived in a nice neighborhood and viewed prostitution as her job. She was polite and reserved but conversational if I got her in the right mood.

Even short-termers like myself got the sense that the shelter system was like the Hotel California made famous by the Eagles—people checked in, but they never really left.

Albert Nolan, a Catholic priest born into a fourth-generation, white South African family, worked many years among the most impoverished people on the continent of Africa. After I had worked cross-culturally in a few different settings, I came to appreciate his cautions to those of us who crossed borders. People who are not poor progress through four stages, he said, when they begin working with people who are poor. Simplistic as any such paradigm must be, it nevertheless spoke to my experience.

Nolan explains that well-off and well-meaning people (like me) who begin work in service to the poor are primarily drawn to such professions by personal compassion. We want to use our gifts to help others. We often begin with relief-oriented work. We give, we simplify our lives, and we connect to individuals.

If we stay at this work, however, we experience a fundamental shift in attitude. We begin to discern—and then become angered—that poverty is a structural problem with deep and resistant roots. As Nolan comments: "Poverty, in the world today, is the direct result of political and economic policies." [1] We try to shift our work to address these fundamental causes of injustice.

Later, we realize that if we truly want to change the political and economic systems that promote poverty, our role as "helper" will be limited. People who are impoverished can be and, indeed, must be the ones to imagine and change the systems that manufacture poverty. We do not have the right—or even the basic insight—to do it for them. They understand what needs to be done in ways that we do not. There may be roles for us to take, but they are not the major ones, and they should be offered and not assumed. This is the stage, Nolan says, at which people of privilege often idealize those who live in material poverty. "We can get ourselves into a position where, if somebody is poor and says something, then it is infallibly true. Or, if somebody comes from the Third World, we must all listen simply because they come from the Third World. And if they do something, it must be right. That's romanticism, and it's nonsense."[2]

Finally, we must be disabused of this romanticism. We will confront the reality that poor and oppressed people, like all other humans, carry faults, commit sins, make mistakes, and spoil the cause. This recognition, Nolan says, brings the first true opening for authentic relationship among people from all backgrounds. Disillusionment and disappointment open a door.

I cycle through this process constantly. This spiral is part of my life.

We cross borders for many reasons, often not by our own choice. But regardless of what drives us into another place and people, if we stay long enough with open eyes, we start to see ourselves.

Why was I there in the inner city? To learn. To watch. To try to understand the world. And, patronizing as it sounds now, to help others if I could. I was there to understand more about people—how they survive, how they love, how they are broken, and how they live past that brokenness. I wanted to use any power that I could channel—faith, education, resources, access to the system, political subterfuge—to heal some of the pain in the lives of others. Yes, I wanted to help.

But even in the naïveté of my twenties, I recognized that structures were part of what determined who ended up in the red-light district and who got spit out of institutions like Duke. And it had much less to do with talent than we might want to believe. So perhaps I wanted to make restitution.

I wanted all people to have the same chance to be good, to live out who they should be, and to find their sermon. I wanted that level playing field. I didn't want the cards to be stacked against anyone. But this dream defies reality. The cards are stacked. Can we stack them less dangerously or less fatally if we really work at it?

We cannot fix all of the world's problems simply by adjusting resource disparity, though that would certainly be a great and obvious start. The real pulse of life and change is always buried in the seeds of relationship. The power of wealth—its seduction and prison— paralyzes our ability to be in authentic and growing relationships across the human community.

It took me many years to find the words that expressed the yearning I felt that summer. They come from an aboriginal activist group in Australia, relayed by Lilla Watson, a member: "If you have come here to help me, you are wasting your time. But if you have come because your liberation is bound up with mine, then let us work together."[3] Yet the task of empowering others and ourselves can be the most challenging, mysterious, and unexplored quest we can undertake. It takes all the courage, wisdom, and stamina we have.

In the Gospel stories, Jesus spends a lot of time in crowds with people who come to him for healing. I find something vulnerable and beautiful in the image of this holy man walking through the countryside teaching, touching, loving, eating with people, and healing. Crowded and pressed by people who want to touch and see him or praying on mountains alone, his story is one lived in relationship. But relying on relationship can be terrifying.

I never brought people in the "inner city" to Jesus. Most of the people I met already knew Jesus well, prayed to him constantly, and found in him the love they had never been able to find from any earthly brothers or sisters. Like many of us, some of them embraced painfully distorted theologies.

Did I think that if these people really "knew Jesus" then their lives would be filled with sudden miracles and success stories? Many of us want, desperately and often out of love, to see that Hollywood ending where the holy man's power makes the boy come back to life and everyone lives happily ever after. The addict is healed instantly (no need to go to AA meetings for the next twelve years), gets his own house, marries for love, and works a good job with the cable company. I love those stories. I celebrate each one. But if I needed one each day to get up and do my work, I'd have left this work long ago.

My sojourn in D.C. taught me that systems do manufacture poverty and that well-meaning help from outside the neighborhood can sabotage the most well-intentioned goal. There is no doubt that people try to beat the system. But it is also true that if the system quit creating poor people and then trying to redeem them, a part of the economic system would collapse. A lot of well-compensated careers depend on poor workers and poor people who need services rather than relationship.

I worked on a magazine called *The Other Side,* and our most reprinted article over forty years was a feisty, groundbreaking piece by John McKnight, a community activist in Chicago. Understanding the power of relationship rather than systems, McKnight made a crazy and oddly wise argument: The best way to fight poverty is to give money directly to poor people. Forget the go-between—the counselors and social workers, the housing program administrators and group therapists, the caseworkers. Assume that people might know best what they need for their families and for themselves.[4] McKnight championed empowerment. Systems of aid are built upon inadequacies and deficits. Communities are built upon relationships and assets. We need to discover how to build on human gifts instead of building on limitations. We needed to lift up the capacities of people—not their weaknesses.

McKnight's thinking alternately upset and intrigued people, and I understood why. His solutions seemed naïve. Yet, we find his concept at the heart of the microcredit loan programs that are transforming many local economies internationally. Women decide what their families need to get on their feet economically. They go to the Grameen bank or some other local institution that grants small loans to poor women who seem like risky investments. They buy their cows, goats, or seeds—whatever it is that might lead them to their dream. And they work those dreams, often as small, relational collectives. Those fragile, little loans have a huge payback rate. This successful model assumes that poor people often know what they need—and we need to get out of the way and let them go for it.

Urban neighborhoods are not as different from rural farming communities as they might appear. In both areas, people will judge others based on whether they are perceived as being from outside the community or inside. In some ways, it's harder to break into a rural community because outsiders are simply not from there and never will be. In contrast, many urban communities are composed of shifting populations. Still, it is not uncommon to see strange and lovely alliances in these places where daily life can be a struggle.

My housemates and neighbors all dubbed Robert Lakeland the "Mayor of N Street." Robert was an alcoholic. Several times I found him passed out, looking like death, in the parking lot behind the house. Each time, I was terrified for him. But when he was up and well, he took a generous and proprietary view of everyone on the block. One fall evening, as I was locking up Bread for the City, a young man I did not recognize materialized at my elbow. He wanted clothes. I was alone, which staff tried to avoid. My coworker Juanita had just stepped on the bus to get home to her daughter.

I explained to the man that I couldn't reopen the building, and I asked him to come back in the morning. My response was not well received. His request came again, and he loomed over me, more threatening. Fear rose in me. I was pondering my best response when I saw Robert lurch up from the steps across the street and brandish a fist. "You aren't hassling her, right? It's closing time. You come back tomorrow. Or I'll come over and take care of you." And Robert started staggering across the street. (I didn't totally approve of his method, but a wave of relief definitely washed over me.)

The man looked, nodded to Robert, grunted something, and walked away. Robert caught my eye and ordered me to get home, as though I was a wayward teenager.

But I wasn't a teenager. I was an infant, and I hardly knew anything.

Chapter 9

Crossing the Rubicon

Allow me to offer the following confession: I have lived by taking much more than my share of this earth's resources, and I will betray my brothers and sisters on this planet for the rest of my life by continuing to do so. I am a First-World consumer, an extremely difficult addiction from which to recover.

To understand this, I had to travel to the other side of the world.

In the mideighties, China was just opening economically to the West through the policies of Deng Xiao Ping. Cultural openings in that decade were not quite keeping pace with these economic reforms. Some years, foreigners were allowed in China with few restrictions. Other seasons, rules and security measures would suddenly tighten. Four years after my stay in China, Tiananmen Square would put a totally different, unforgettable face on the idea of "letting one hundred flowers" of thought and perspective bloom.

To get to China, I had to do my part in spreading imperialism and globalism. I went as an English teacher, part of a specifically Christian program that sent teachers in teams all over China. It was against the law to "proselytize" in China. The program simply wanted to make Christianity appear credible in China at a time when most Chinese viewed it (and any religion) as akin to worshiping rocks or Santa Claus.

I brushed off my set of cultural rules—(avoid foreign ghettoes, learn the language and history, speak as little English as possible, listen, and remember that I don't even understand that which I am sure I understand.) China made following most of these guidelines difficult. I found it impossible to immerse myself fully in the culture. For one thing, society was structured with a type of apartheid for foreigners like me. We had our own (monitored) housing and ate in a special, separate dining hall. We were expected to patronize a special systems of "Friendship" stores, train-waiting areas, and hotels. These were more comfortable, vastly more expensive—and very isolating.

Most North Americans and other First-World compatriots, accustomed to comfort, were rather petulant guests. The water heaters didn't work or were unreliable. (Very few Chinese households had hot water at the time.) The flush toilets were never cleaned properly. (People cleaned for us.) Squat toilets were the source of endless discussion. (People don't really outgrow their fascination with potty issues.) The heat (set at about 59 degrees, tolerable if you wore layers, as Chinese people always did) was never adequate. (Heat was turned on by date and date alone—on November 15 and off March 30.) The light bulbs were too dim; clothes had to be washed by hand; the food was too monotonous (meaning it was always Chinese—go figure).

In China I learned the following cardinal rule: People always look up the economic and social ladder to make their comparisons and not back at those above whom they stand. Because of this, we are almost never satisfied with what we have. With a paycheck of 600 yuan a month, I made ten times what my students made, and unlike them I paid nothing for utilities. This was true even though most of my students were ten or fifteen years older, taught college classes, and had families to support. Yet I still heard other foreign teachers with higher salaries complaining of "low pay" and pointing to other foreign teachers who made more.

I brought home from China a sense of what it means to live in a conserving economy intensely mindful of resources. Though its economy was beginning to emerge, and with it some material comfort, China was only one generation removed from scarcity. It was still a developing country, even if Marxism had leveled a few of the extremes of wealth and poverty in its history. And although it had accomplished this good, the control that accomplishment needed bore problematic fruit. I left China with mixed feelings toward capitalism, socialism, and Marxism. All have significant problems and blind spots.

China desperately wanted to move out of the "developing country" category, even though some parts of the country had significant poverty. It bore all the schizophrenic marks of an economy desperately transitioning—bustling cities with four-star hotels (for foreigners) and countryside that yielded food through massive human labor. I lived and taught at a leading science university in Beijing—hardly the hinterlands. One afternoon after class, I sat at my desk in the classroom and looked at the plain, functional chairs and tables, the dirty concrete floor, and the walls painted in the ever-present pale green, the institutional color of choice. A dusty February wind howled outside. The back window had one pane missing, one of many reasons that I never went to class wearing fewer than five layers. I heard a slight rap at the door, Mr. Hu, one of my undergraduate students, probably eighteen, entered the classroom.

Mr. Hu, often quiet in class, seemed to be a loner outside of it. His thin face was covered with acne and shone eerily pale under strands of hair that were straight and oily. His teeth were bad for his young age—crooked and yellow, visibly swollen gums. (One of the sure markers of poverty, at home or abroad, is poor dental care and hygiene.) He was prone to terse comments that were neither kind nor complimentary, though they were often true, usually followed with silent bouts of laughter that shook his slight shoulders. I always paid him extra attention, knowing how awful it feels to be isolated in your class.

That afternoon, Mr. Hu asked a grammar question and a question about idioms, which I quickly answered. But he seemed to want to linger and talk. First, he inquired how I liked being in China and what I thought of my time there. This led to a longer discussion of differences between our two countries. There was a lull in the conversation. He looked out the window, clenched his small hands, and turned back at me. "China used to be finest, strongest civilization in the world—we invented gunpowder, paper, and a sophisticated writing system. Now everyone thinks China is poor and backward." He locked my eyes. "But I tell you that China is going to be great again very soon." With a small, upraised fist and a slight, almost fanatical grin, he continued, "We will rule the world!"

I looked into Mr. Hu's eyes, pondering nationalism and all its faces. I thought of all the things that I loved about his country—precisely because it was not rich. I loved how I bought my single serving of morning yogurt in gray pottery containers and returned the container when I bought my next one. I liked how drinks were sold in little glasses, quaffed on site, and then left with the vendor. I loved the string bags everyone carried to the daily markets and the close honesty we had to the food chain. If family members planned to eat duck that day, they usually brought home a duck and put it in the bathtub to be killed and cleaned later in the day. My North American generation was dismally ignorant about the agricultural and animal rhythms previous generations understood and lived by. In China, we got what was in season.

I loved people having just a few pieces of clothing and practical shoes. I loved the basic packaging and the almost total absence of marketing. I liked to see the streets thronged with the best sustainable and energy-efficient transportation method ever invented: the bicycle. All ages, from one-year-old children to ninety-year-old adults, negotiated much of the world from that perspective. I loved joining the sea of navy-and-gray-clad riders going where they needed to by using their own muscles. I never tired of what human ingenuity could pack on a bike—tables and chairs and even a sofa!

I loved walking into a store for a product and not being overwhelmed with options. If I needed laundry detergent, I saw at most three options, all packaged in plain cardboard containers with blue writing on the side. I remember this when I stand in the grocery aisle in the United States, scrutinizing shelves that sport fifteen kinds of Tide detergent, let alone the other twenty brands with all their permutations.

I call to mind the account of a woman from Eastern Europe who walked into a grocery store in the United States for the first time. She looked at aisles groaning with multiple offerings, the meat counters spanning the back of the store, the cold, air-conditioned produce section with its timed water spritz—and burst into tears. When I do not numb myself, I feel incredulous grief at the opulence, the options, and the incredible waste.

My student Mr. Hu looked at all the ways that China did not glitter, glow, buy, sell, and dispose like First-World economies, and he felt shame. I looked at the same and felt a strange hope and relief. I looked at how seasonal vegetables and fruits cycled through our diet, how water and electricity was conserved, how trash for the week fit on one dustpan—and I felt inspired.

Most Chinese people with whom I spoke understood the vast scope of resources China's large population would consume, even if people kept their needs at a modest level. To adopt a policy restricting each couple to one child was unimaginable, yet most people understood and at some level accepted its rationale. They lived with the reality that those in the United States do not: Natural resources are limited, and living within these limits demands significant constraints individuals must accept. Cultural norms in China emphasize the needs of the group. Children are taught from an early age to sacrifice individual preference for the good of the entire family or community. This perspective has defined China for centuries and puts it in stark contrast to the individualism of our own culture.

I witnessed the dynamic of group orientation in my students when they made decisions about where to go for the afternoon, how to study, or who would go first in class. A subtle process of one person feeling out what others wished to do, checking the lay of the land, played out in each instance. How disparate were opinions? How could all come together?

I think of myself as a "group person" in the United States, but in the context of China, I discovered my inner lone North American. I felt like the most selfish person on earth with my constant need for solitude and space and my love of traveling into neighborhoods alone rather than in pairs or groups. I failed to pick up on group expectations or felt constrained by them. I continually approached group process with the North American solution, which is to split up and let the people who want to do Y go in one direction and the people who wish to do X go the other. We find a linguistic clue to the chasm between US and Chinese cultures in the absence of a Mandarin word that parallels the Western sense of *privacy*. Mandarin culture does not revolve around the fundamental of respecting individuality. Coming from the United States, where our inability to put constraints on individual impulses and choices might just end up sinking us, this mind-set was very refreshing, even if it did make me crazy. It was a good crazy, and I needed the lesson.

This is the Rubicon my culture finds so difficult to cross: What shall I give up for the common good? How much of what I *could* grasp for me and mine shall I deny myself? I sense very little willingness to do with less. Like those expatriates working in China, we are fixated on comfort. Yet, if we are to address climate change and the environmental crisis seriously, curbing consumption and doing with much less than our parents will be required. If we cannot go there, we will be unable to meet the needs of a world in ecological crisis with any real imagination.

Historically, China has a less than well-developed ecological sensibility. Environmentalism has not been part of the social equation. The (much deforested) land, tilled for thousands of years, was viewed as a system of production to manage and not an ecosystem to protect. Ethics of conservation have been spawned by frugality rather than sentiment for the natural world. Some of my students had spent parts of the Cultural Revolution plucking every blade of grass and ground cover from under trees. Grass was considered bourgeois; bare dirt was better.

After my first year of teaching, I moved into a Chinese household for three months. My Chinese housemate, her friend, and I took a camping trip. Camping was a new option in China. At least where I lived, Chinese culture was not much of an outdoor culture. Only a handful of areas in the country allowed camping, and it was executed with a unique twist.

I had brought a tent with me to China, a fact my students greeted with curiosity and consternation. After I had explained how camping worked in my country, they looked concerned. "Teacher, we don't think it's possible to do that here in China—to just go in the country-side and stay. If we had to travel without knowing anyone, we would just knock the door of a peasant and ask for a place to stay. Perhaps you could do that."

My housemate knew my longing to be outside, so there was a look of great satisfaction on her face as she told me of a newly developed tourist site where people could actually camp. We plotted our outdoor excursion for weeks.

To get there, my housemate, her friend, and I got up at 4:00 a.m., rode our bikes a few miles with heavily loaded backpacks, and caught a packed bus to take us to a crowded train. We arrived around midday at a small village under the stony white mountains of Hebei province, just us and one hundred other teenagers who were planning the same outing. We hiked en masse over a muddy trail through several rice fields before reaching the campground.

On our way, I had spotted a flat area next to a cornfield, one lone tree shading it, a river nearby. "Let's pitch the tent here!" My camping mates' reaction was immediate shock: "But nobody is around! We are completely by ourselves!" I should have known.

The camp was a large, cordoned rectangle about 100 feet by 200 feet. On every side were open fields. Inside the cordoned area, identical red pup tents nudged up against each other in rows as tight as human imagination could stake them, with a water pump and sparse cooking facilities in a corner. It looked like a refugee camp. My heart took a nosedive.

"I can't do this," I whispered. "Maybe we can find another spot." Though clearly anxious about leaving the red tent village, my housemate and her friend were willing to wander down the river to please me.

A small river wound through the valley, shallow and filled with stones. It was summer, and the rainfall had made the often dry valley green and lush. Neat, small fields clung to every spot of level ground, and the small houses clustered along the river were built from what the land had to offer—the rounded, sun-bleached stones, mud, and clay. It would be a difficult land to wrest a living from, but we were tourists, and the quality of our lives did not depend on that daily contest.

I found a spot along the riverbank that was dry and less rocky. The sun was dying in the west as I set up the tent. We ate our bread and tried to coax a flock of ducks along the bank of the river into sharing it, but they swam on, melting into the evening quiet. A few minutes later, they came back, swimming frantically. Hot in pursuit were five teenage boys throwing stones at them, tourists like us from the city. This was not a First-World country, so this was not the game of bored teenagers. Half an hour later, the boys trudged back up the river to our bank, carrying two dead ducks. They cleaned and roasted them a stone's throw from our tent.

It must have been midnight when I heard the low, mournful cries of a farmer calling, calling. He had spent the last dark hours searching for the two ducks that had not returned home that night. We recounted to him what had happened and fell back asleep.

My housemate and I were up before dawn, and he was back as well, staring desolately at the river, kicking through the blackened ring of coals that marked their campfire, searching for any clue that would help him find them. We knew that he never would.

That flock of ducks was a key part of this small, subsistence farmer's life. He had wasted over half a night searching for two small birds. Those of us who do not raise our animals or plants for food have no sense of the value of each fruit, each animal. Once we become detached from that connection to land and food production, it becomes easier and easier to dispose, waste, and pollute the earth that feeds us.

My experience in China comes to me every time I read Jesus' story of the rich man and Lazarus. In it, Lazarus, the poor, leprous beggar, lies at the rich man's gate every day, imploring him to offer crumbs of food and leftover coins. The rich man never notices him. It is a story true to human life. Chasms of human experience divide us. We find those chasms not only across economic systems but also within them. The ducks were simply one more example of that dynamic— the farmer for whom laying ducks meant nutrition for a year, the city kids who come into his world on holiday and destroyed that security, I who had never killed a live animal with my own hands for food.

Musimbi Kanyoro, a native of Kenya and former world secretary general of the YWCA, shares the tension of working on behalf of women in poverty while living in a technologically driven and wired culture in her article titled "Living Across the Chasm." She describes speaking with women in Zambia who spend every daylight hour hauling rocks—baskets of stones they load onto trucks—while minding babies and toddlers. Upon returning home after a trip, Kanyoro found one thousand waiting emails from "'the city,' place of 'electricity': urbanized or semi-urbanized settings where it is possible to access televisions, telephones, and all the tools of modern communication,"[1] and she must answer them. "A chasm lies between us," she confesses of herself and the women for whom she advocates.[2]

What will ever bring our worlds together? Is it possible to bridge such gaps? I returned home from China with those questions burning inside me. I prayed that it was possible; I dreamed that it was possible.

Chapter 10

One Wild and Lovely Life

My return from China confronted me with the extreme culture shock of moving back to a materialistic and disposable consumer culture. Fresh from a place where "taking out the trash" meant depositing one dustpan of refuse weekly in the community trash pile in the courtyard, I felt smothered by North American affluence and waste—the lights burning; the heaters and air conditioners constantly running; the forests flattened into clean, white, wasted paper; the immense barrels of trash hauled to the curb every week; and the insatiable tarmac eating up green spaces for cars to hurtle everywhere on fossil fuel. I was disoriented by the individualism of a culture where people made very isolated choices with a shallow understanding of interdependence. I craved the group dynamic that had smothered me in China. Any conversation with my elders explored one of two tired topics: What was I going to do as a profession and was I seeing anyone special?

I scrutinized the nice, safe lives around me. The people I knew seemed to construct good lives by finding a community or church they liked, buying a house that they could make their own, spending their weekends working on it, seeing family or friends (normally from school, work, neighborhood, and church), and usually having children.

My friends and family found a richness, a simplicity, and a certain satisfaction in these pursuits, yet I felt restless, looking in from the outside. *Is this all there is?* I asked myself. *Is this what we are all living toward—species perpetuation? Is the point of life to live comfortably and to offer that opportunity to our children and our children's children and so on?* I was searching for something deeper and more vital than a good job and a comfortable life. I was listening for a pulse—that instant connection between strangers and the sense that we are joining hands to make a world that is stronger and in which it is easier to live compassionately. I was looking for love, community, and faithfulness. I was also looking for a way of life that might teach me.

In her poem "The Summer Day," poet Mary Oliver asks the haunting question: "Tell me, what is it you plan to do / with your one wild and precious life?"[1] This is hard enough to answer when we actually *are* living for something. But if we've only built our lives around our homes, our families, our day jobs—how will we survive when those disappear? (Bet on it—some of those aspects are going to go.)

We carry some choice in what our lives become. Depending on accidents of birth—culture, family, personality, and access to resources—the space of that choice can be almost infinitesimal or more spacious. As a pale, blue-eyed child born to middle-class parents in the United States in the second half of the twentieth century, I had the privilege of many possibilities.

Yet there are limits. We only decide some things. We are also shaped by the forces around us. Poverty, illness, cultural norms, ethnicity, and class are defining (and often constraining) backdrops, even if they are not definitive molds. We all must find some way to get our essentials—food, clothes, and shelter. Every day, we must negotiate our loving and wounded relationships with one another, and we find our needs within the jungle of our wants.

I've spent a lot of my life trying to learn—and then accept—what I can control and what I cannot. I do have one conviction: All my life choices should be shaped by my hope, by the lovely outline of what I am dreaming this world to be. My life transitions—almost always painful and uncertain—have usually led to the experiences that have carved and shaped my holy room. Dreams came to me in that holy room, each one offering something to hope for and live toward. Each was like a lovely, variegated window set into that simple holy space that offered me just enough light—a single oil lamp on a small home-made table. The holy one came, sat in that room, and asked me to say yes. And sometimes, I have said yes back.

I dreamed of a world with a more equitable distribution of resources, where sustainability was a primary value and materialism had lost its addictive power. I was acutely conscious of an earth reeling with waste and ill-conceived, unnecessary consumption. I wanted to live a different, more nurturing life, rooted in a specific land and place.

I dreamed of a world of widespread authentic relationship, where the best resources were not distributed along color and class lines. I yearned for a world incapable of embracing extremes, where children no longer die of starvation while others die of obesity related health issues. I thirsted for a world where race had finally lost its power so all that remained was the intriguing diversity and breadth of human cultures.

I wanted men and women to find the work they loved in the world. I had grown up in a house of women, all now grown to be amazing, strong, and wise. I wanted a world that gave them as much space and breathing room as it gave its men. I wanted a world where gender no longer determined social role or status. I wanted men to be good cooks and caregivers, fielding the calls about the carpools and play dates. I wanted women to be able to fix cars, build houses, and not have to shave the perfectly good body hair with which they were created. I wanted the decision to have children not to cost women so disproportionately what it cost men. I wanted those who felt that male-female gender paradigms did not fit their embodied experience to be able to live into their own identities and loves.

I wanted relationships that were deep, intentional, and faithful. I wanted women to love whomever they wished completely and over time. I wanted men to love whomever they wished completely and over time. I wanted a culture less hooked on physical beauty and more infused with love and healthy sexuality. There is not enough committed and working love on this planet, and there can never be too much. I wanted children to be raised well and whole and wise out of such relationships.

Most of all, I did not want a world that insulted and tainted me with its tolerance of poverty and pain. I did not want to bear witness and to participate in allowing the wants of the wealthy few to devastate and suck the very lifeblood of the many. I wanted to lay my life right down in that awful chasm between the wealthy and fattened and the poor and famished and scream, over and over: "There is a bridge here. We can build a bridge!"

Were these dreams large at the core or simple? Could they be both? The prophet Isaiah had a beautifully compelling image of contentment and life—that each person live under his or her own vine and fig tree, a simple but radical vision. What I wanted was a world, in the words of theologian Peter Maurin, "where it is easier for people to be good."[2]

When I left China to return to my home in the states, these dreams seemed enough around which to build a life. I realized that it would be a life lived largely against the culture in which I was raised. It was not going to be "successful" in the currency of that culture. As Duke classmate Paul Farmer, who has worked in Haiti and elsewhere for these last three decades, comments: "We *want* to be on the winning team, but at the *risk* of turning our backs on the losers, no, it's not worth it. So you fight the long defeat. . . . I don't care if we lose. I'm gonna try to do the right thing."[3] I couldn't agree more. I was willing to release that old seductress—success—in order to live with more integrity. I desperately wanted to live into my dreams. I hoped I was willing to pay the cost.

I began working at a Christian magazine in Philadelphia called *The Other Side* and settled in the urban neighborhood it called home. The organization had long shared resources between Christians in the global North and those in the global South but wanted to build more substantive partnerships rather than merely funding relationships. For someone coming out of the developing world, who was distressed by consumption and materialism, the job was perfect.

They asked if I could make a two-year commitment to the job. I gulped and agreed. It seemed like a long time to stay in one place and a very long distance from that piece of land I loved in South Carolina.

For the second time in my life, I settled into a struggling urban neighborhood. Most of the neighborhood's white residents had fled in the sixties and early seventies. The flight to the suburbs and ongoing disinvestment had left their mark on the community—a collection of row houses in various states of abandonment or repair and the usual small economies of poor neighborhoods: small bars, mom-and-pop shops, take out places, check-cashing joints, secondhand stores, and repair shops. I was back in the city—a place to which I never expected to return.

The Other Side magazine was founded in 1965 by Fred Alexander, a white Baptist preacher aghast at the silence of white Christians in the face of racism. All that was needed, he believed, was a voice to rally the troops. He decided that voice would be a homegrown magazine cranked out on an old, secondhand press in his basement.

The first issue was downright ugly. It sported a few tiny, posed, black-and-white photos, and its few illustrations smacked of the worst church-bulletin clip art. It was packed with passion and intention and didn't give a hoot about how it looked. After all, the world was full of important things to take on: racism, militarism, sexism, economic justice, soon to be followed by the environment, gender issues, human sexuality, immigration, and AIDS.

The founding staff was serious enough about "walking the talk" around race and economic justice to relocate from small-town, white-bread Ohio to a struggling urban, and mostly African-American neighborhood in Philadelphia. They moved into an abandoned building and rehabbed it into a mostly functional but ratty office space. Most of the staff lived in that same neighborhood. The organization's modest salaries were all equal, with an extra stipend available based on the number of dependents in each staff person's household, rather than position or seniority in the organization. "Living simply" in a world of consumerism served as the core value of the organization.

The Other Side tried to live outside the mainstream. It did that imperfectly—very. But the magazine wanted to experiment with alternative models of living. It worked to build a staff community. Employees could use a shared organizational car, took mandatory all-staff coffee breaks to build relationships, and attended regular voluntary prayer times and Friday afternoon happy hours. Maintenance and chores were rotated. And at one point or other, everyone cleaned the bathroom.

The magazine became more visually appealing over the years but retained its no-nonsense, gritty personality. It talked a lot about "costly discipleship," and for many who worked there, including myself, it *was* all about cost; about an activism that asked something sacrificial in the name of justice. This activism included forgoing our wants in a world fraught with injustice and poverty.

My work with the magazine content both thrilled and challenged me. Articles took sobering looks at flawed principalities and powers—the military industrial complex, the criminal justice system, race distortions in all their manifestations, how the free market works and its victims, and the lust for power and innate greed in human hearts. I listened to the stories of Christians who had been through horrific experiences of poverty, abuse, repression, war, and torture in the United States, Guatemala, El Salvador, Haiti, the Middle East, the Sudan, China, and Korea. There were heartening stories of courageous faith communities worldwide who incarnated amazing biblical possibilities.

Those who worked on the magazine were highly invested in it. Unexpectedly, I became as invested as the rest of them. The work dovetailed wonderfully with my skills, my values, and my life. I met my soul mate, Will, there, and after we had supported each other as friends through a few romances and breakups, we decided that we were utterly in love with each other. We still are. The lives I encountered in that work spanned the globe and reshaped my life. This great stream of witnesses fed my vision and stoked my courage.

I remember a moment in the late eighties when I sat in a sunlit room in Guatemala City, frantically taking notes as I listened to a white-haired priest tell the story of his life. Outside his office, I saw the afternoon sun shining over the city. It caught on the towers, domes, Castilian architecture, and commercial sprawl of the business district—a district that drew in people during the morning and spat them out in the afternoon, some to the wealthy districts and suburbs, some to squatter shacks in ravines. The light held some of the particular brilliance of a country full of color and so much pain.

The priest's eyes, blue and equally brilliant, held that pain as they sought my own. As he spoke, his words had that rare quality of living wholly, without fragmentation and contradiction. His lifestyle and values spoke the same tongue. To hear one was to envision the other accurately.

The priest had come to Guatemala City as a young, Spanish-speaking foreigner. Eventually, he was run out of three communities because of his work with the poor. Finally, he left the church, left his vestments, and found his life anew among the people he had tried desperately to serve from within the church structure. He settled on a corner of land in the unyielding Guatemalan highlands and became a subsistence farmer, along with a vast majority of people in that country who in good years coax just enough corn and beans from the earth to keep from waking with hunger at night. Only then did he begin to understand power and poverty. Only then did he begin to understand the church.

> The poor taught me to speak, live, and love. They taught me a respect for human beings I could not find as I grew up. They taught me to plant. They told me of their mythology and history. From them, I learned of the strength that lies not in structures but in poverty.
>
> We talk about the poor as though they were a place. A neighborhood. That is a grave mistake. The poor are not a place to work or evangelize. Poverty is a place we come from to speak of God. . . .
>
> The poor do not have at their disposal the forces of power. And that is their salvation.
>
> Our temptation on this earth is to use power—to dominate, manipulate, and control people. As we live in this world,

this is what we constantly, consciously or subconsciously, try to do. . . .

Here in Guatemala, and all over the world, there are three forces that destroy people's lives—military, industry, and the church . . . . Christ did not pray "Your church come" but rather "Your kingdom come."[4]

The priest continued, reminding me that the reign of God is here and now, worked out in the stuff of our frail yet resilient lives—and nowhere else.

There are, in life, forces which are not scientific nor determinable—birth, death, and faith. Our confirmation and our hope lie exclusively in how we see and live life. Faith is not an abstract question. It is a history; a gesture. It is action carried out. The gospel is not in our minds. It is in our hearts and in our stomachs. . . .

Human life is precious, and we only live once. Life is a free gift of God. You have only one. Put it behind things that matter.[5]

After the interview, I stepped into the mellowing light of the Guatemala City afternoon, conscious of a call to reweave my own life in a pattern that was closer, tighter, and more whole. "That's it!" I whispered. I yearned for a life with integrity. Choose a side. Fight the long defeat. Yield over to it that single, wild, lovely life.

PART III

Of Gifts, Loss, and Persistence

*[The Shunammite woman] said, "Did I ask for a son from my
lord? Did I not say, 'Do not deceive me'?"*
2 Kings 4:28

*We do not choose a gift; it is bestowed upon us. Some gifts we
accept, some we do not understand, and some we fear.
Some of the gifts we have feared, we grow to love. Some of the
most longed for gifts crumble in our hands after we attain them.
Many times we question whether we are worthy of a good gift.
Must we be worthy of a gift?*

The Uses of Sorrow

(In my sleep I dreamed this poem)

Someone I loved once gave me
a box full of darkness.

It took me years to understand
that this, too, was a gift.
—*Mary Oliver*

Chapter 11

Tell Me Something Real

A s the story of Elisha, the Shunammite woman, and the hospital-ity that they offer each other unfolds, fresh dreams come. And so does the unimaginable.

> [Elisha] said, "What then is to be done for her?" And Gehazi answered, "Truly she has no son and her husband is old." He said, "Call her." When he had called her, she stood in the doorway. Then he said, "At this season next year you will embrace a son." And she said, "No, my lord, O man of God, do not lie to your maidservant." The woman conceived and bore a son at that season the next year, as Elisha had said to her (2 Kings 4:14-17).

The story takes a turn. Elisha confers with his servant, Gehazi. What is to be done for this woman who asks for nothing? Her husband is old; she has no son. Flush with the power of God, Elisha promises the Shunammite a son. (We do not know if she has a daughter. The Bible contains many unnamed daughters.) In a patriarchal setting where women's status and survival hinge on having men to care for them, Elisha is offering this woman security for her future.

The Shunammite is taken aback and is less than polite. Her unexpected response is a kind of a foreshadowing: "Man of God, do not lie to me." She has built the room, following a call with no sense of where it was going nor any expectation of the holy man. She has followed the urgings of hospitality. Because of this, unexpected things are born into her life.

Yet the Shunammite woman does not ask for this son. The others decide, believing he will be good for her life. Who would not welcome this news—especially a woman facing the prospect of widowhood in a patriarchal economic system? Her primary response seems to be fear and the desire to protect herself from the pain of unfulfilled promises. *Don't lie to me, holy one.* There is no worse pain than when promises we believe to be sanctioned by a greater, wiser, and stronger power falter and fail.

Similar to the Shunammite's story, my spiritual path brought new passions to birth in my life. Led by the insights and sometimes-enigmatic stories and sermons of Jesus, I became excited by how one person, individually and as a part of a community, can live out genuine alternatives to the dominant culture. For me, this has meant thoughtful, intentional work on issues of race, lifestyle, gender, and parenting. These are large dreams. I did not give birth to them, and they are not completely my own. My passion is life-giving and carries the power of birth. It makes me feel more whole, more connected to my brothers and sisters. It strengthens my belief in prayer and the powerful healing of the Spirit. An unexpected life comes to the Shunammite, and an unexpected life has come to me—a life where there is work to be done, work given to me. This book is about this unexpected life with its visions and birthings of dreams and the reshaping and sculpting as we live into them.

But that is not the whole story. The Shunammite's child dies.

When [the servant] had taken [the child] and brought him to his mother, he sat on her lap until noon, and then died. She went up and laid him on the bed of the man of God, and shut the door behind him and went out. . . . When she came to the man of God to the hill, she caught hold of his feet. And Gehazi came near to push her away; but the man of God said, "Let her alone, for her soul is troubled within her; and the LORD has hidden it from me and has not told me." Then she said, "Did I ask for a son from my lord? Did I not say, 'Do not deceive me'?" (2 Kings 4:20-21, 27-28).

This is a story of searing grief. This woman requests nothing from the holy man, and he gives her a child. Then the child she has not asked for, who nonetheless burst into her world and changed it, dies suddenly and inexplicably. A hole that would have never been there is open, raw and gaping.

This spirited woman doesn't take that sitting down. She sets out for the holy man, and she doesn't stop until she finds him. She brushes by his aides and office managers, his spin artists and flunkies with the same phrase: "I'm fine. Everything is fine." She holds her burden, those waves of grief and anger, until she can weep over Elisha's feet. "Did I ask you for a son? I told you not to deceive me!" She refuses to let Elisha send his servant to deal with the problem. She is a woman made bold by intense grief. The holy man wants to send Gehazi, but she resists. She's taking the holy man back with her.

When we move into new parts of our lives, there is a place for grief. There is a place for deep, intense loss. Those things that God makes possible that we know are the work of God are not invincible and can still be destroyed. I believe we have to be in touch with our grief when those works we are called to do fail. Here, much of our theology does not help us.

As I write this—during midlife—I am thinking about dreams and death. I am too much in the Shunammite woman's story. I was forty when I birthed my first child, a son. I was forty-two before my second, a daughter. When they came, my covenant partner and I had already given substantial years to work we felt good about. We had strong commitments to building community in our neighborhood, to working toward housing persons who lived on the streets of our city, to working for organizations and publications that inspired people to be their best selves. It was work that felt good to our hands and suited to our gifts. We wanted it to be part of building a better place in one small corner of the world.

But things died. Making the choice to be in one place—and a fragile, sometimes broken place—does gradually make other choices less possible, not only for me but also for my family. I have seen a number of dreams die untimely deaths. Some things that I believe I was given to do have died in the worst way, right in my lap.

I have no idea what to do with a dead dream in my lap. Now in the middle of my life, I stare at it. But in the story, the woman carries that death right into her holy room, the place she made for the holy man. She lays it down, stark, on the bed, shuts the door, and goes to find Elisha. When she does, Elisha orders his servant to go to her house immediately.

Then [Elisha] said to Gehazi, "Gird up your loins and take my staff in your hand, and go your way; if you meet any man, do not salute him, and if anyone salutes you, do not answer him; and lay my staff on the lad's face." The mother of the lad said, "As the LORD lives and as you yourself live, I will not leave you." And he arose and followed her (2 Kings 4:29-30).

Chapter 12

The Woodshed of Grace

In my twenties, I wanted to find something larger than myself to stand behind and throw my life toward. But I am older now, and I have learned that to have a dream, especially any dream large enough to hold my life, is to also wake up at night and glimpse failure. It is to grope in my sleep and feel suddenly—and with a shock—the certainty of loss. It is to see parts of myself I do not wish to believe are there. There is no breaking apart the companions of failure and loss. They are wedded. Yet, I do not tell myself stories of failure. And my inability to tell them becomes my inability to live as fully and richly as I am able.

One image from the Christian tradition is Jesus' quiet reassurance, "My yoke is easy and My burden is light" (Matt. 11:30). A more accurate translation of Jesus' idea in this text about the yoke is *fitted*. We can imagine Jesus saying, "My yoke fits you; it is for you alone, so there is some ease that you have in it that no one else does."

Often, older people make fun of young idealists—or the dreams of their younger selves. They imply that relinquishing big visions is a good, mature thing to do. I believe that the most essential work we have to do in this world is to marry the hope and vision of youth with our failures. This work allows us to become who we are meant to be. It releases a wiser, stronger power in us that will sustain us for the long haul. We cannot tap this power if we do not face and share our failures.

Certainly, some people are successful. From the outside, their stories read like fairy tales. Yet somewhere in their authentic story is the real stuff—their confrontation with their failed humanness; their loss, inadequacy, and inability to be who they wish they could be. Life breaks some of us sooner, some of us later.

For decades, I lived a charmed life. My work was satisfying and used my best gifts. Despite ups and downs, I was part of a workplace with a strong community ethic. I am deeply in love with my covenant partner. My husband and I chose to live in a struggling neighborhood because we wanted to join our neighbors in making it stronger. We were integral parts of an organic garden in the community. We started a space for serious, disciplined scripture study that continues after twenty years and has touched many lives. We lived simply, hosted various intentional worship groups, and met committed, amazing Christians from all over the world. Our lives felt unremarkable—but whole—and connected to things we cared about.

As the years rolled on, life became more challenging. My husband and I had two children in our forties. I appreciate the complex challenge of parenting, but I'm not very good at it. My workplace imploded in an incoherent mix of conflict, scarce resources, and distrust. I could see all my control issues, micromanagement, judgmentalism, and failures hanging out. (Except for when I couldn't, which was worse.) My poetry wandered out into the world and got lost. I watched myself, my growing children, and my partner, realizing that we would be a family who lived with funny wirings, learning disabilities, and depression. My body got older. My old rental house was always in ill-repair and untidy. Life came to teach me of loss, of limits, and of failed experiments. And that is how life began to sculpt me into my most authentic self.

Henry David Thoreau left a haunting description of the way many of us live our lives: "The youth gets together his materials to build a bridge to the moon, or perchance a palace or temple on the earth, and at length the middle-aged man concludes to build a woodshed with them."[1] I spent midlife wondering what I had built. For anyone not in pure survival mode, this is a midlife preoccupation—taking stock.

My vocation, which was also my paid job in the world, withered away a number of years ago. Overnight I went from feeling competent to feeling the opposite. I began to doubt my skills and myself. I began to snap at my loved ones and my children. I sometimes needed coaxing through my days. A close friend offered the following trenchant and wise assessment: "There is simply not enough contentment in your life."

We live in a world saturated with a mandate to succeed—to which I was susceptible. Before I lost my job, I felt successful. And in a quirky, social activist kind of way, I had been. In a niche of the Christian world, the voice of *The Other Side* was respected, and I was associated with that strong voice. Professionally and in other ways, I have wrapped my sense of self-worth around accomplishments, even while perfectly aware that from a spiritual perspective, that was a dangerous, proud, and inauthentic way to live. My faith in accomplishment has come back to haunt me.

I come from a long line of doers. All of my working-class ancestors lived by the following mantra: You rise to work; you go to sleep when you are exhausted. We link our merit to the speed and clarity with which we complete tasks. But in midlife, I read stories of people at the top of their game, and they are younger than I am. At night, I stared into the face of jealousy, and jealousy became my own face. This had never happened to me. I had never wanted to be anyone else. But such discontent can come when we lose our place and footing in the world.

In addition, each day confronted me with the difficulty of living with integrity in this world and the energy it demanded. Most products—from food to clothes to cars to electronics—are made in ways that consume the earth, both in their creation and in their disposal. Making different choices can take everything we have, and almost all of us are forced into some compromise. If we truly embark on cultural resistance and minimizing our global footprint, such cultural resistance will quickly consume us and become the place from which we live.

Such resistance seems impossible without supportive community. Apart from connection to a like-minded community, making different choices about neighborhoods, schools, marriage roles, parenting, jobs, salaries, and consumption can be terribly isolating. Without others accompanying us, our good intention to build a world on alternative values is doomed.

I have discussed these issues with others at my stage of life, where many aspects of our lives are already defined. By midlife we are supposed to have figured out our occupations, and most of us have logged decades of experience in them. We've often worked our way up whatever ladder was presented to us. Most of us have had kids if we wanted them. Often, these children have progressed well into their own lives. We've located our home, neighborhood, city. Many of us have chosen partners. Some of us have chosen to be single, are still single, or have divorced and chosen again. We have let go of dreams from the past and lovers from whom we are permanently separated. We have released the vocations we considered but did not pursue because of life's demands, because of how others saw us, or because of our own fear. We have children with whom our relationships are strained and disappointing. We have forsaken visions that needed help from others, the hopes that illness or struggle took down, the dreams we didn't try because we were old enough to fear failure too intensely.

Our twenties and thirties are full of new life and experiences to savor. We explore partnership and love. We try our hand at work. Many of us move into the consuming experience of parenting. In those early years of adulthood, many new frontiers lay before us. At that time in my life, I felt like I was using my whole self. But the passage of time changed that. No longer working out of my strong suit, I saw myself riddled with issues and incapacities. As life unfolded, it confronted me with the inescapable tension between two truths: the undeniable reality of change and my need for something to hold onto. We cannot live well and healthily while at the same time willing everything to stay the same. Staying the same is not the nature of life.

Change may be our rich and heady friend when we are young, carrying us into new experiences and new roles and new loves. Eventually, though, change is marked by beautiful possibilities quietly slipping from our grasp to become part of the past. In midlife, I began fighting a childish and ultimately destructive battle against change. I was holding on to things of the past. My children were no longer infants. My vocation was gone.

Of course, all such resistance is totally doomed. But that resistance helps us face the latter truth—our need for something steady. We need ground that is changeless. We need a framework capable of holding our lives steady enough to weather change, and every day we search for it. Choosing what is steadfast demands that we discern our hopes. Those hopes need to be large enough to subsume our lives in a larger stream of human endeavor. The best of our work as humans, in fact, is finding our place in that stream. When we develop an awareness of our place in the flow—of who came before us and our trust that someone else will come behind, we give ourselves over to change but still feel our feet on solid ground. Finding our place demands familiarity with failure and intimate knowledge of our vulnerability and weakness.

If we are growing into wisdom, failure can become our guide, our learning place—that bend in the stream that allows us to glimpse the way forward. What we imagine as failure perhaps is not. What if Thoreau's woodshed is actually the useful and appropriate thing? Perhaps we do not need to build a bridge to the moon.

When I moved to Philadelphia, I stumbled upon a house church whose members, most of whom were old enough to be my grandparents, gave me my most riveting life lesson. I was able to share parts of their emotional and experiential lives as a friend and community member. They gave me this single life lesson: Even the most ordinary human life is filled with tragedy, loss, and failure. Perhaps this does not seem like rocket science, but at the time, I was two years shy of thirty. Totally unconsciously, I believed that if I listened to my heart and lived my values, if I had a decent education and any social currency, then I had a fair chance of avoiding extreme pain and tragedy.

At that time in my life, I felt that deep loss, wrenching tragedy, and life-rending circumstances were more the exception than the rule.

In the house church, I found a community of folks who also experienced great loss. Most of them were financially secure, the majority from stable backgrounds of privilege. Many were successful and highly regarded in their professional worlds. They were thoughtful about the values around which they oriented their lives. Most of them seemed to have chosen life partners fairly wisely, sometimes after a first mistake. They had all raised children to adulthood. They loved God and neighbor and tried to live well. And yet, over time, I began to see the tragedies—the daughter who had drowned at two with the whole family around; the father who had fled the family with young children, leaving intransigent wounds around abandonment, lack of money, and fear of intimacy. Stories of childhood abuse; emotional desertion by parents; mental illness in children, parents, and spouse; financial collapse; unemployment; and utter poverty after the age of fifty. Illness, disability, and death. Failed marriages, incarcerated and addicted children. Every person had wandered a path of pain.

Some of these losses had scabbed over and healed. Some broken places had even grown back stronger. But many wounds were still raw, peeking out only when someone took a deep breath and decided to be vulnerable. Just glimpsing these losses and failures created a deeper bond among the church members, even when we recognized that a hurt still lurked, untamed. These companions gave me the gift of realizing that we are all in this life thing together and taught me that getting to the other side was not going to be easy.

Aging is a story of release and choices. Some will call it a story of loss. It is a process of giving ground to the generations that follow, and while this is lovely when we are still in charge, it becomes sharper and more threatening when younger people are doing jobs we used to do better and with more vision. At its best, aging is a story of learning to see gains in new ways. Aging forces us toward new language to talk about the latter half of our lives.

In the first half, we anticipate what lies ahead, ready for us to try. We are going to be great lovers, parents, workers, world-changers. We have a vision of the lives we will live, and we often imagine that vision unclouded by health issues. But in the latter half, we feel less certain. We are not as sure what gifts we have to offer, and people are not so willing to take them. People reflect truths about ourselves back to us, and the truths are not always welcome. It is painful to mature in a culture fixated on youth, and yet we will all do it.

I finally realized the importance of sharing our stories of death, loss, and utter failure. I love those Hollywood stories of hope and triumph, where the underdog finally gets the big break and things inexplicably work out. I've lived a good number of such moments. I have seen the lone Chinese demonstrator after Tiananmen stand in front of the tanks. I've been part of grassroots neighborhood demonstrations that defeated powerful political machines against all the odds. I believe, foundationally, in change that comes through joining hands and moving forward toward small—and incredibly heartening—successes.

But those are largely not the stories we live. We eke out the human journey primarily in start-and-stop, inch-by-inch ways. The many compromises made along the way leave us feeling unsteady. Yet as I have aged, I have realized the power of telling these stories. Our stories move beyond paradigms and into raw human connection, shaking our convictions and drawing our solutions into question.

Many years ago, a poem about confession came to me:

The forgiveness of sins is perpetual.
All our lives—
the bloom, the bruise,
the gentle swell and tear—
all our lives are the creation of some eternal and fantastic
fruit, color and shape never seen before;
born from the forgiveness others have offered us
and we have offered others—
space for our terrible, beautiful unknowing of God.

Confession helps us turn from our vast unknowing of God toward understanding. The word *repent—teshuva—*means "to turn," so as to aim the arrow true to the mark. I like the gentle redirection implicit in that concept. No big wrong or huge mistake. There is nothing that cannot be redeemed. Instead, I often whisper to myself, "This path isn't working. Sit still. Think creatively." I will try something else and go a different way. This reminder offers peace. I want to reclaim the powerful function of confession as release. I want to gather that power into my own life and share it with my community.

What follows are my stories—stories of knowing little, taking much, and misunderstanding. Stories of confession offer absolution, but done well, they remind us of grace, joy, and the ways we can be made more whole. They can be tools of conversion. Confession offers us the gift of imagining ourselves responding differently in certain situations while at the same time reminding us that most of us do not always act like the people we would like to be. When received with love and grace, our confessions can actually lead us toward our dreams. They can lead us to our true voice and power. Perhaps the function of confession is to help us say real and vulnerable words to one another.

Here are my confessions of dreams that I have betrayed, of failure, of times when I have not been the person I want to be. The older I get, the more I wish to tell them. When we glimpse grace in those moments in which we feel like failures, we are so much more likely to become stronger healers.

We have to be real with each other as much as possible. We don't have time for anything else. After all, the world stands at our doorstep with all of its daily struggles and challenges. We need the light we can kindle from sharing our hopes, our dreams, and our failures. So let the stories begin. Let the door to healing open, and let grace pour through. The Shunammite kept her room spare and open with only the essentials—bed, table, lamp.

As I approached the threshold of fifty, my life partner, Will, penned me the following note:

Your Jubilee year.
Part of the meaning of *Jubilee* is "home gathering."
Let us seize the hope that you are beginning a journey
back to the true home of your heart.
I will go with you.
—W.

Chapter 13

Bed, Table, Lamp

Confessions on Marriage and Family I

Will and I hiked through a small path in Switzerland, winding through pastures with golden-brown cattle, stepping into mountain forests of fir and evergreen. In late October, the afternoon sun fell like something palpable, like gold poured across mellowing green pastures that pierced shrouded forests with lances of light. Our quiet conversation changed the trajectory of our separate lives. Both single and in our thirties, we were deciding if our futures belonged together. Our answer to each other was yes. We knew the cost would be living a very different life together than anything we could have imagined if we remained single. Days before our wedding, my mother sat on my bed, looking out the window, her brilliant blue eyes pensive as she searched for the words. "Dee Dee, marriage is simply a different life." She paused. "It is not a change in one's life. It is bigger than that. It ushers in a completely different path, and you, in it, become a different person than the person you might have become as a solitary woman. You and Will have chosen to make this life together, and every dimension will be different than if you had not."

I never expected to marry, even into my thirties. My vision for my life did not include a partner. I was full of dreams about my future, but for the most part, the life and future that I envisioned was solitary. I thought my life would be full of art and words and many friends and independence and the ability to choose my path unfettered by negotiation and compromise.

When I consider the weaving of my life with Will's, I still cannot fully take in the intricate pattern of change and compromise. Our life together has meant living in a city rather than a rural area. I live in a part of the country and do work I had not imagined. Our intertwined lives brought me two children in my forties who reshaped my perception of myself. This life has brought me different communities and friends and interests than I expected. That other, solitary life that I had imagined now belongs in the unchosen past.

During my first few years of marriage, I felt as though I had a secret. I rushed home from work thinking as I opened the door, *He's going to be here, in the place we share—these two rooms, this garden, this life.* Will's presence always seemed like a miracle, a quiet spring of joy spilling into my very ordinary life. I couldn't grasp the wonder that I had found him and that he was there every day with his listening eyes, his piano music winging throughout the house, his keen mind, his humor and writing self, and his love of me. Eight years later, when we had a son—and later a daughter—I felt again that giddy sea of joy rise and carry me. Every homecoming meant stepping over the threshold into an indescribably joyful life.

But those same years were wrenching. Will and I brought unknown and unexamined patterns from our families of origin into our relationship. We thought that we knew each other, only to come home and find a stranger pacing the house. Nothing could have taken us by surprise more than these strangers who ambushed us in our own home. We were not ready for them or the costly compromises they demanded.

I was a control freak who could run Will and myself both ragged constantly creating endless, exhausting possibilities. Will found himself reacting to me as he had his father, a man who was given to yelling. We struggled with core questions about where to live (rural or urban?), what our vocations should be (farmers, writers, teachers, community builders, all?), and whether to have children. We each projected our own passions on the other. We spent long nights contemplating whether our choices were too different to stay together.

I found a small, scrawled journal entry I wrote after a painful discussion about our future:

> I look in your eyes, searching for spaces of compromise. I lie next to you, unsure of what I am grieving—the life I will never have, the life you will not have. I stand at the window a long time, listening to the whine on asphalt and watching the life I have never lived move away.

Several years later, after Will and I had children, I wrote the following:

> My beloved is having a bad day. This is a euphemism. To be real about it, he is rocking in bed, fighting demons that have spent all night whispering to him in dreams more real than his life. The demons put their hands deep in their pockets and pace the floor, telling him that he is incompetent, that he does everything wrong, that my children and myself would be better and happier without him. He is lying there, alternately believing them, fighting them, then wondering how he should bring an end to this, free us all.

Will suffers from chronic depression, which leaves its mark on him, our relationship, and our home. Our day-to-day rollercoaster ride with depression has gone on for fifteen years. Thankfully, days like the one I wrote about are rare. But we live each day in the shadow and possibility of this illness and its spiritual, physical, and mental manifestations, all brought on by unknown things— seasons, conflation of unexpected stresses, the mysteries of brain chemistry, powers and principalities, twists of DNA strands that go back for generations.

At the beginning of our marriage, there were so many things we didn't know. We did not realize that depression was part of Will's family legacy. When family members pass the age of forty, an alarming number have confronted that cold and bitter Irish wind blowing through their souls. It is a demon, and it aims to destroy.

When Will and I share our struggles with others, we invariably meet with openness and relief. It's shocking—and troubling—how many live with depression or other mental illnesses in beleaguered silence, as if it is some taboo secret. The cultural stigma is palpable.

Depression has left its mark on Will's life and my life in many ways, not the least of which is on our relationship with each other. A friend of mine had a spouse going through cancer. As the long path of surgery, chemotherapy, and radiation unfolded, as friends surrounded the couple with support, he gave of himself consistently for more than a year. He confided with a sigh of resignation, "Her cancer trumps my everything."

I understand. Many of us whose balanced relationships have morphed because of caretaking and illness recognize the frustration and anger of being the household glue, the one who always makes it better for everyone else. We know how this can alter and damage a relationship. Sometimes I am the understanding partner, sometimes I am borderline abusive in my martyrdom, and sometimes I am the abandoned child who no longer wants to take care of anyone.

Yet, I have my own demons, and if anything, they are growing fiercer with midlife shifts. My marriage was wounded by my workaholism that runs deep and springs from an unhealthy desire to please others. I've begun to own the difficult pieces of myself—my need for control, my codependency and lack of focus, my fear of failure, my desire to please. Arriving at the realization of how my own unhealthy patterns created the difficulties that I'd heretofore blamed on others was revolutionary. I no longer saw myself as a victim but recognized my complicity in my own frustration. The prospect of unlearning these deep-set patterns proved to be more daunting than coming to recognize them in the first place. It demanded a kind of dismembering of my identity. I was forced to let go of many wonderful images that I had of myself. I loved those images; I wanted to be that person! But it was time to learn about my authentic self—who I am and who I am not. This is terrifying work.

But if I fooled myself about who I am, I never fooled Will. He knew those parts of me. He glimpsed them even before we covenanted those years ago, and he still chose me.

If my flaws and Will's illness threw our marriage roles off-balance, childrearing took them to the ground. Will and I have always been extremely intentional about avoiding gender roles in our relationship, especially with tasks that take no innate aptitude. Sharing household tasks equally was a cornerstone of our relationship. It was important to both of us that we share cooking, cleaning, growing food, washing, folding, minding kids, and paying bills. We both wanted good work outside the home, but the stresses of parenting put these ideal balances to the test—a test we have mostly failed. We've tried many options to balance work and family to no avail.

For several years after the birth of our first child, Will served as the primary caregiver while I brought home the paycheck and health care. After our second child, we began sharing one full-time position—in many ways the most balanced experiment we had. Then we both worked part-time at different jobs, which was completely unsustainable. For a few years, we resorted to a more traditional arrangement with Will working full time as the primary breadwinner and me at home, a model that we had both resisted.

Will and I tried to share our daily tasks, alternating who got up early with the kids and who put the kids to bed. We struggled to balance home, work, church, and simple living ethics (gardening, buying secondhand, and cooking from scratch) that took time. A vision of an orderly household haunted me, but our small, rented, two-hundred-year-old home in the city was nothing like that. It was in disrepair, gathered dust and bugs by the hour, and the yard was a weed incubator. Sharing childcare and wage jobs was both fulfilling and awful.

Will and I were not always clear about which responsibility belonged to whom as we shared childcare, home management, and garden-tending. We both felt responsible for everything.

Will and I also hit our personal parenting limitations. No matter how philosophically we were committed to sharing tasks, especially those done traditionally by women, we had to factor in temperament. My diffuse attention span proved useful with young children or extreme multitasking but was less helpful moving major projects forward. Will's characteristic single-mindedness made me fear that children under his supervision could wander out the door undetected but made me envious of his efficiency. Our commitments to do gender "right" created internal tension. We wanted to be able to live our ideals, but ideals can be relentless drivers.

Will and I knew these issues were larger than us. At my desk at the magazine, I edited and reviewed fifteen articles by men for each article or book by a woman. I knew one reason I didn't have articles by women was because women picked up so much of the daily support that keeps the world in place—the home, the cooking, the child-care and eldercare, the relationship-keeping, allowing men to retreat to their offices and institutions and make their mark.

My spiritual director listened to me bemoan my family's balance problem as I tried to envision sustainable and palatable options. I sabotaged each workable solution she offered with some moral or ideological conviction. ("Maybe you could find someone to help with the cleaning" she suggested. "Well, we don't have money for that, and I'm not willing to pay someone to do my cleaning, especially since I'm paying them because I am able to earn more per hour than I have to pay them," I responded.) I was unwilling to pay someone for my responsibilities (how white middle-class of me); I was unwilling to make more money (our salaries should be enough). I resisted anything but completely shared tasks with Will, even though we clearly had differing abilities and aptitudes for different kinds of work.

My spiritual director's eyes brimmed with tears. "Dee Dee, you have to be able to grieve. At one level, you have more options than your parents did, but those options carry tremendous costs. You will not be able to live out the ideals that you feel called by God to live out. You will not feel that you are living them in the way that you should. You need to weep over this, as Jesus wept over Jerusalem. Weep long and hard! But then you need to listen to God, who knows you so well and will help you find the path that is truly yours and truly Will's to follow. It must be your own, built from your deepest recognition of who you are." Then she paused and looked at me. "And recognizing who you are will mean accepting who you are not. This will be difficult."

Stepping into a commitment of love over time—whether that be to partner, a friend, or a child—places us at the beginning of an unknown path. Part of that path will always trace the edge of abyss, a place of loss and grief, because the presence of love immediately introduces the inevitability of loss. Not all old wounds and the wounds we inflict on one another will heal. Some will defy healing despite our best efforts. But if we are honest about them, they can teach us things we could not otherwise learn.

Love is a gift Will and I decide to give again every day. We offer this gift in spite of illness, depression, and the tyranny of the mundane. In spite of failed dreams, paths abandoned, and some wrenching deaths. In spite of weeks when one of us struggles with demons, rocking in our bed. In spite of our horror at who we can be—hard-hearted cynics or sellouts in the culture, greedy and exploitative consumers in the world, explosive, unwise, and controlling parents, faltering followers of Jesus. Still we return always to that pool of mercy and love.

Wendell Berry's poem "Marriage," describes two partners hurting each other and then turning to find healing. Its closing line reads as follows: "It is healing. It is never whole."[1] That describes many parts of my life beyond my marriage—my parenting, my work in the community, and the shadow depression and my own penchant for control laid over our lives. We are always seeking to heal and to be healed. We are never whole.

Chapter 14

Parenting, Privilege, and Loss

Confessions on Marriage and Family II

I began parenting in my forties. Words cannot express my love for my children. They are the souls I have been able to see unfold in all their complexity, lives I have truly been able to attend to. But having children has been costly. Parenting has taken a toll on Will and me. It has shattered paradigms we held about the world and ourselves. It has triggered complex emotions from our shadow sides and changed the shape of our marriage and partnership.

The stakes of parenting are high. Wounds we inflict on our children—by impulsive reactions or by not deeply listening—are real and lasting. I believe in a Spirit that has the power to drench our hearts in a sense of belovedness. But I also know that the places where we have not been loved well will show themselves, and our old wounds and brokenness will leak out onto those whom we desperately do not want to damage. This recognition has made the experience of parenting terrifying. Will and I often joke that our responsibility is to give our children therapy issues. Isn't that what parents do?

I watch my friends with their parents. How many of our parents treat us as other adults do—namely like the engaging, thoughtful, flawed adults we are? How many adults do I watch interacting with their adult children and think, *I want that relationship with my adult children?* Almost none. How can I, a flawed parent if ever there was one, possibly beat the odds?

I write my children a journal. I'm not sure when I will give it to them—possibly when they turn twenty-one or possibly never. In it, I record moments I want to hold onto and many that I would rather forget. In many ways, it serves as my explanation for all my parenting, good and bad. I talk about why my husband and I chose to live in a poorer neighborhood than we could afford and why I sent my kids to a particular school in spite of the fact that they were in an extreme racial minority and seen as "different" in other ways. I write openly about moments I did not even understand in my own parenting, when I was so frustrated at one of them that I did not recognize myself, that yelling woman. (Perhaps I will give this journal to them after they have parented a two-year-old. Parenting a toddler teaches us a great deal of mercy, forgiveness, and understanding for our own parents.)

My friends reassure me, "Oh, c'mon, you are a great mom." I know they think that. I think that about them too. We all know just how impossible the job of parenting is. Sometimes I cannot repress the refrain that has become my parenting mantra: "We did the best that we could."

What Will and I didn't realize until we were one week into parenting is that parenting is a political minefield. I used to describe myself as a *nuclear* mom (read *explosive*) because in the parent circles I frequented, I often felt like the only mom close to blowing her top. In those circles, parents were not supposed to get angry. If they did, they were supposed to keep their voices matter-of-fact and bright. These parents were masters of diversion and gave their children choices. Some of them had spent their entire lives working for peace and nonviolence in their communities, and they responded gently to their children's requests. They never spanked their children. They were guilty of what my own parents termed, with some derision in their voices, "negotiating with their kids." In my parents' eyes, negotiation was akin to being an ax murderer. Worse, really, because it insured that they were raising ax murderers.

Me—I snapped orders and expected obedience. When really pressed, I parted company from these parents with old-school responses such as, "Because I said do it or I am going to spank you." And sometimes, I did just that. I would raise my voice. I have called out my children in front of friends.

These are confessions; I am not proud of this behavior. Before children (BC), I prided myself on my patience and ability to see every side of a complex question. My children unlocked all the hidden anger I carried from being a good girl all those years. I wanted them to be good too, and when they wouldn't, I got frustrated.

My parents lived in a different world when it came to relationships with children. Children existed to do what you said, when you said it. Children did not ask why. They did not demur or offer their own assessment of a situation. A proper parent did not offer children another option that they might find more palatable as a pathway to procuring their obedience. All of that was paving the way to hell.

My firstborn is like me—stubborn to the spine. Luke is a kid who would rather die than be controlled or told what to do by anyone. He doesn't go in reverse—on principle. As a small child, he was not the kid around whom you placed a boundary. Instead, I constructed the Berlin Wall. People didn't understand how much energy it took to build the Berlin Wall several times a day. After a while, I whittled those boundaries down to the essential ones.

Luke was about one week old when my mother gave me a copy of *Dr. Spock's Baby and Child Care*, the classic parenting manual of her generation. Perhaps it was one of the first of the genre. (Before that, I gather people did not read books about raising children. They got their advice from one another and from grandmothers.) My mother also gave me *On Becoming Baby Wise: Giving Your Infant the Gift of Nighttime Sleep* by Gary Ezzo and Dr. Robert Bucknam, a book written because they believed a lot of fine young (Christian) mothers were being taken in by the philosophy of attachment parenting. (Being good liberals, Will and I already had William and Martha Sears's book *The Attachment Parenting Book: A Commonsense Guide to Understanding and Nurturing Your Baby* on the shelf.)

The Sears's premise on attachment parenting was that forging a strong parental bond fostered confident, capable, and well-adjusted children. Mothers nurse their kids "on demand" (as often as they seem fussy or might be hungry) and tend to breastfeed longer and take their kids everywhere they go, often attached to their bodies by slings (necessitated by the breastfeeding). Those practicing attachment parenting often co-sleep (where the infant sleeps in the parents' bed at night). Pacifiers are strongly discouraged. Schedules are loose, and the word *schedule* itself is viewed with suspicion. The child is not put on the parents' schedule; the parents are put on the child's schedule.

Baby Wise authors, on the other hand, wanted to set those supposed heresies straight. They are big on schedules. From day two, babies are put down at a designated naptime so they can learn to put themselves to sleep. *Baby Wise* parents practice a strict "cry it out" policy. The authors believed that attachment parenting philosophies propagated exhausted mothers and spoiled, whiny children.

I stuck my copy of *Baby Wise* next to my copy of *Attachment Parenting* and *Dr. Spock*. I read them all and became mostly confused. The manuals seemed to stress that if I did the wrong thing, my children would be marred for life, misfits, and burdens on society—all terrifying thoughts. As a result, I was schizophrenic in my childrearing—some moments all law and order; other moments conciliatory.

Will and I quickly learned that child rearing is neither a biological function nor a spiritual discovery. No. It is a political issue. Child rearing paradigms are imbued with the same political frameworks as our religions, our political parties, and our economic classes. *Baby Wise* reflected the values of a conservative worldview—the child is molded into the world. He or she must fit into the family. And, of course, this is how we raise good Christians. *The Attachment Parenting Book* mirrors the values of liberal and progressive worldviews. Children should be viewed as individuals. The goal is not to fit all children into one mold but to value each child's differences and allow for pluralism. And, of course, this is how we raise good, spiritual people who can choose their path, perhaps even choosing to follow Jesus. I am a proponent of "good enough parenting" like those of us who aren't really cut out for the impossible job before us. I hope that telling my kids I love them about one hundred times a day will cover a multitude of sins. There are a multitude of sins to cover.

From the outset, the visceral loss involved in parenting has haunted me. Parenting is about pouring ourselves into another life that we know will leave us. One night, when Luke was not yet two, I suddenly realized that he had disappeared. I quickly searched our small house. No child. Although we lived in a densely populated urban neighborhood, our yard connected to another one with a twenty-foot drop—plenty of space for a small child to get lost and seriously hurt. I was terrified.

I ran into the night and yelled to your father, "Do you have Luke!?" My voice was shrill with fear, picturing you on the long dark path between the houses or in that old, cracked pit we should have covered months ago. I heard his anxious cry coming back, your father who hates to raise his voice. "No! Where is he?" We ran into the darkness from different directions, two parents running into their worst fears.

I almost tripped over you. You were standing at the open gate to the big yard, teetering on the top step. You were looking out to where your father had gone, into the night. You knew you had done a bold thing—slipping out of the screen door by yourself and going after him—and you were frightened by where your boldness had brought you even as you were excited by being big and by your sheer love of being with your father.

So you stood in the half-light shivering, unwilling to return and yet afraid to proceed. On the horizon winked the moon through traced branches. On the horizon, calling like sirens, was adulthood, maturity. All things.

This is how we venture forth into life. Love and some compulsion to move into our own launches us into unknown reaches and then we are afraid, uncertain when we should come home and try again later. This is the dynamic we live with—the going out and the coming home—and even now, *after many years, I cannot say whether the joy is the going out (the anticipation, the exhilaration mixed with fear) or the arms that carry us home. We go out, I believe, so that we can come home.*

When I had children, I realized that my parents love me more than I love them. This came as a shock, but it is true. It cannot be otherwise. As a parent, I carry a powerful, unmatchable love for my children who came to me so vulnerable and utterly dependent. I am not able to return that kind of love to the generation that bore me. The consuming way that a parent must love a child, the kind of intense love and attention required to raise him or her, can only be offered forward to the next generation. The realization that underlying the admonishments, advice, control, and criticisms of my parents burned the same raw and incredible love I carry for my children was startling. I began phoning home a lot more often.

This intense love, this desire to give our children the best possibility of becoming who they want to be raises the two-edge sword of parenting for me. I care—fiercely—for my own children. I also care deeply about building a world in which all children can access good nutrition, education, and basic healthcare. I want each child to know what it means to be loved.

Yet, I parent in a world channeling all its best resources to a few children—and little to the rest. Within my own country, I see the vast disparities. International settings present an even more extreme situation. Parenting has the capability of perpetrating great inequality and injustice, in part due to structures we keep in place for the benefit of our own children. Parenting flings each of us into the jaws of this soul-shattering question: What and who am I willing to sacrifice so that my children live well?

Our selfishness on behalf of ourselves is bald and evident. We know those instincts and can even distinguish between those meant for self-preservation and those designed to gain advantage. But our selfishness on behalf of our children becomes much more complex because it is also a measure of our love for our children. We want to do everything possible to make sure that they live happily, that their lives are not scarred by problems, that they achieve their best potential. We desire to give them every advantage. We are rooting for them.

I ran into a second cousin at a nonfamily-member's wedding, the coincidence of webs of connection. I had not seen her since childhood threw us together, this child of my father's first cousin. I knew from rumor that, like me, she saw the world differently from her father. She handed me a different version of my childhood seen through her eyes. "You know, I envied you. Your parents were always there, cheering you on, cheering you away from home if that meant you followed your dreams. I wanted that." My eyes fill with tears. My life had been upheld and nurtured by parents who cheered me on in the best way they knew how. We need these voices that stand behind us, insisting upon and drawing out our strongest selves. Whatever differences lay between us, my parents wanted to do that for me.

In many ways, the most revolutionary shift in the religious script offered by Judaism and later Christianity was the image of God as a parent—a God who loved us, chose us, and yearned for ongoing relationship with us. To worship a God imbued with the emotional connection of a parent and a parent's desire for us to grow and do well was unprecedented and incredible.

Nonetheless, seeking every possible advantage for our children hints at the shadow side of the love that we bear for them. For here is the inescapable and ugly truth: The playing field is not anywhere near even. Our world is weighed down by structured and intentional inequality. One child's gain comes at the expense of others. Of course, anyone can die young, fall sick, or be hurt. People do not possess equal ability, and they have different potentials. But we live in a world where, beyond this, advantage is fashioned and strategized. Some children are favored over others, and we manipulate whatever we can to see that our own will be among those favored with enough. Enough food, shelter, health care, education, love, success.

Last night, your father and I took you to a prayer service in the city. The world has gone lunatic—wars in Afghanistan and Iraq. We went to pray for peace.

In the front, huge posters of the real victims of war—other children—displayed the cost of war in human flesh, in scars of powder and radiation, in bloated bellies.

You got restless. I opened the snacks we packed so you wouldn't be "hungry." I stared at children with bloated bellies who were older than you but who looked much younger, children who had probably already died. A family of five sleeps under a blue tarp like the one I bought at the hardware store to cover your sandbox. The sandbox sits behind our house, mostly forgotten, with the tarp blowing unnoticed in the wind.

You looked at the posters and asked me, "Mommy, what happened?" How could I answer?

You asked me where the mean people are, and I tried to explain that there aren't really mean people and good people. It's much more complicated. You asked me what war is. I could think of no answer except, "It is never playing ever again."

You played with all the toys in the church hallway, getting them out, then leaving them. In your world you always have more toys.

This is the juggernaut of our age—we know the inequities and yet feel so powerless to cast them out. You and your children will look at us and at all we might have been able to do and wonder at our impotence. You will turn to us with your wide, questioning eyes, and we will not have an answer.

Later, we picked up the pictures pasted on posters and walked them into the rainy winter night where a circle of people will sleep in front of City Hall in the cold. I did not dress us for the weather, and you were soaked. Your sister had no socks or hat; the stroller canopy dripped on her sleeping head. I felt awful—guilty, angry at myself for not protecting my children. The greatest pain of all—and no one carries it more than the refugee—comes when we cannot protect our children. To not be able to shelter, feed, clothe one's own child—that, Luke, is hell. And our world is constructed so that many, many parents live in it.

So many of us come from a place in the First World in which we know we have too much. We realize that our answer to "What is enough?" is so skewed as to be laughable. I believe that the ways of the world can shift. I believe that two children do not have to starve in the time it takes me to write this sentence on a laptop that costs ten times the amount of money either would have ever earned in their lifetime had they survived. In my simple mind, the shift hinges on our ability not to be selfish for ourselves or for our children.

We may find it difficult to be unselfish for ourselves. But to be unselfish for our children is almost impossible.

Sometimes it seems that the world contains two kinds of people: those who never see children die and those who watch children die every day. These two types of people almost never cross paths. I can count the number of dead children I have seen on one hand, each one lying lovely and loved in a coffin. Incredibly, horribly sad, and yet different than a child's body shot and lifeless on the street, beaten in a back alley, starved in a barrio, shot crossing a river in El Salvador, or attacked by lions as he or she, a small orphan, crosses the deserts of Sierra Leone.

Mothers in my neighborhood fear a day in which they might hold their dying sons in their arms. Mine is still not a community where young, black men are assured of growing to old age. Nothing is assumed. I have seen two young men shot thirty feet from me and knelt by one as he bled to death on an icy January street.

Each year, a few whimsical and haunting totem poles of stuffed animals rise up in my neighborhood. Each marks a place where someone was murdered. At every site of a fatal shooting (it is almost always an African American male between the ages of thirteen and thirty), people start piling stuffed animals. Bears and other animals are attached to telephone poles, parking signs, meters, or piled in doorways. I used to dwell on the irony that these young people, most of them less than half my age, are memorialized by such a childlike symbol as stuffed animals. But it is real and right. They are all children made to grow up too fast. These totems of animals provide a metaphor for the childhoods some children in these vulnerable neighborhoods will never have. The totems stay a long time after each incident. The acrylic fur grays in the elements, the sun bleaches the ribbon collars, and the stuffed animals sway limply in the wind. Then one day, the totems are dismantled, and the landmark disappears.

A dead body lies in the Shunammite woman's holy room.

No matter what other dreams, prayers, and healings have occurred within the walls of that room, she cannot escape the wrenching reality of a corpse. The Shunammite's son dies in her arms, and she carries the body upstairs and places him in the holy room.

God sends her a son as a gift for her faithfulness—this is not a child for whom she has asked. The child is a direct gift of God, and he comes wrapped in all that God stuff—the sheen of miracle and grace, the shout of hallelujah, the disbelieving joy of realizing that her deepest desires are known to God and that God yearns to fulfill them. Gifts like that carry a sense of eternity and therefore invincibility. When this gift—unbidden and bestowed with the certainty of blessing—dies, she must confront something terrifying. So must we all.

Chapter 15

The Second Touch

Confessions on Race and Class I

When I transplanted from the South to Philadelphia, I settled in a block of row houses, and I still live two blocks from there. Then and now, most of my neighbors are working-class and poor African Americans. I've often heard the following maxim, sometimes attributed to civil rights leader Stokely Carmichael: "Your politics are shaped by what you see out of your front window." I find this blunt statement to be true. My windows looked out on two decaying, boarded-up houses and a struggling community garden on an abandoned lot.

A prayer group on my block gathered weekly. One evening, I brought up an incident. Several nights earlier, I had seen a young kid I didn't know run up the block and into an alley tailed by four police officers. I was completely unprepared for where the conversation went.

"I always tell the young people, 'Whatever you do, and no matter how scared you are, *don't run*! That makes the police mad, and they will take it out on you.'"

"Whenever the police chase someone behind a house, I holler, 'Bring that child out here where we can see what you are doing!'"

Each person in the room had a personal story of victimization or misuse of police power, mild or serious. One recounted how his son had been falsely arrested coming home from church and accused of an Ohio bank robbery. Another, a big proponent of Romans 13 and respecting authorities, described how her son had been wrongfully picked up, and how she had followed the police car to the station. "I wasn't about to let them take him in that station alone!"

A father told how his son had been pulled over several times when driving the family car, a new model. A mother shared how she discouraged her kids from wearing popular styles of clothing. "I tell them that if they wear what the other kids wear—same hoodies or shoes or T-shirts—they'll be picked up because they match someone else's description. Once the police have a suspect, they think the case is solved."

Only I, the sole white person in the room, had no story to share. And I admitted to no one but myself that when I mentioned the police chase, I was fishing to hear what the kid had done wrong.

Until that night, I believed errors and mishandling by the police and legal authorities to be occasional and largely isolated incidents. My neighbors were committed Christians and upright people—not political radicals. They still looked for change through personal conversion instead of addressing policy. I naively believed that households like theirs—highly religious, scrupulously moral, obedient to authority—would be served by the law enforcement system as I had been. I believed that the fuzzy areas of abuse I heard about largely occurred in households with murky, ambiguous relationships to law and order.

The Philadelphia police will probably never pick me up for the crime of a woman who does not remotely match my description. I won't get pulled over for driving a nice car. Police officers come up to me at night in certain parts of this city to ask if I need their assistance. My ongoing conversion from racism is predicated on hearing again and again the unconscious privileges my white skin gives me. Only over years and with the gradual relocation of my life have I begun to discern the ubiquitous pass that privilege hands me. Though I have structured much of my life around living out racial reconciliation in some incarnated way, my whiteness will not let me go.

By most real and tangible measurements, my vision of racial reconciliation has failed. Much of my world and my closest circles remain predominantly white. I try to work in racially integrated groups, but usually one group dominates. I haven't been able to find or create language that doesn't follow all the stale, tired paths of most contemporary discourse on race. I want words that bring people together in hope and real cooperation. This language has eluded me.

I have lived in this predominantly African-American neighborhood for more than twenty-five years, but to the degree that the neighborhood itself has a fabric, I recognize that I am not fully in the weave of it. My kids didn't hang out on the block with other kids and I don't really enjoy block parties enough. At some point, class and race divisions play into our neighborhood relationships. I am still affected by being raised in a culture that saw race first and individuals second. For example, I remain weak at cross-racial recognition. It is not unusual, especially in larger groups of people of color, for me to need to hear the name of a person of color four or five times more often than I need to hear a white person's name to remember and place him or her.

My friend Carolyn and I were talking after the kind of meeting I attend all too often—a group of people committed to faith and social change where the crowd of white faces is broken up by a smattering of African-American faces. (I also find myself in the reverse situation often enough. What I rarely experience is a racially balanced, empowered, and well-functioning group.) Carolyn was accustomed to being one of a few people of color in the room, but she usually emerged weary and discouraged by the subtle race and class barriers she had to negotiate. The fact that everyone meant well didn't spare her.

As we left the meeting, she commented, "I know I was asked to participate as a way to 'diversify' the group, but it's just too draining. One thing I've observed—you white people seem to use your work together as a way to create relationships. African Americans work differently. We need strong extant relationships to do the work."

That was Carolyn's last meeting. I'm sure no one ever thought her absence was due to subtle racial barriers in the group.

Though many of us are aware of racism and how it operates, our communities and coalitions often experience breakdowns due to intangible and ill-articulated obstacles. Carolyn's insight was one of many reflections on differences that come into play. What makes easy, honest, and fluid working relationships across race so difficult?

Unrecognized cultural norms play a significant role. I carry a lot of habits that spring from a dominant culture of whiteness and middle-class-ness. I like things organized on paper and with written language rather than feeling comfortable with a more fluid, oral culture. I find relationship with others through work and task, just as Carolyn pointed out, instead of using relationship as a way to come to tasks. I'm very time-and-task focused, at the expense of being more adaptable and relational. I'm heavy on analysis and perfectionism and light on action. I find speaking my opinionated mind to be easy, and I may not make space for other voices who take more time to find their place.

I believe that guilt—about race, privilege, anything—plays a large role. Guilt has its good sides. It reflects the sense that our actions do impact others, often in ways that are not just. In that sense, guilt can create a primal recognition of connection, springing from a sense of relationship that might not have been perceived before. But guilt also exists to transmute itself. Guilt flashes up as a messenger, urging us to restore right relationship. When all goes as it should, guilt gives us the momentum to take restorative action. However, that's not always how we respond to guilt. Instead of using guilt as a catalyst for constructive action, we often latch onto guilt as the destination. Guilt becomes a spiritually paralyzing force.

I see myself and many other whites manifesting this guilt—and unintentionally shutting down significant racial dialogue and reconciliation. Take a situation in which a person of color suggests that my actions may be informed by my racial conditioning as a white person. This is a helpful observation to work with, but often, my white guilt and deep shame at exhibiting a white blind spot make it impossible to do the necessary reflection and correction. One of my mentors comments to me, almost in awe and with a gut-wrenching laugh, "White Christians do guilt like no one I have ever seen! It's incredible. It brings them to a crushing standstill every time so that nothing gets resolved. Any healing process is immediately short-circuited by a battery of lament and self-flagellation."

Most of the white participants in faith-based, social justice groups grasp the injustice of racism, and this understanding becomes their great stumbling block. I, along with other white people I know, sometimes act as though those *other* white people have a lot of race work to do but that largely we ourselves have left racism behind—a naïve belief in the United States at this historical juncture. The troubling realization that certain comfortable behaviors—how often I voice my opinions, whose opinions I interact with, how long I maintain eye contact with certain persons, and who I seek out for conversation in a room—also are imbedded with dynamics of race and class gives me much pause. One measure of victory over racism will be the ease, depth, and authenticity of relationship across race (or class) boundaries. Being truly "color-blind" when it comes to race is impossible since we cannot ignore the backgrounds that shape us. Those backgrounds include race, culture, and economic assumptions that we constantly need to scrutinize.

My friend, who grew up dirt-poor in North Carolina, never understood white Christians. "The Bible says to help people," she explained. "Anyone could see my family didn't have enough money to even buy shoes, and others had so much. But no one ever tried to help us."

One night my friend and I attended an interracial discussion group for faith-based folks who wished to work together across racial lines. More typically than not, the white participants dominated the conversation at such meetings. Unexpectedly, my friend called out that we sounded arrogant. The honesty of her remark rocked the group, especially the white attendees who found the comment unjust. The people of color in the room, however, nodded in agreement and support. They were all too familiar with the assumption that accompanies those of us who are part of the dominant power structure:

Whites can always be assured air space. Before that class ended, we conversed about the ultimate power of race—the power to frame ideas and opinions and the assumption that people will listen to the dominant race's point of view.

My history of resistance to race divisions and stereotypes is unremarkable. Nonetheless, I have persisted despite not getting it right. After decades of working toward reconciliation, I still find it extremely hard to locate and participate in healthy groups that are fully integrated. Dr. King's "Beloved Community" is a very elusive dream to incarnate, even among groups for whom antiracism is an explicit commitment.

But some places have met with success. One of the most successfully integrated neighborhoods in the nation is Philadelphia's own Mt. Airy, a mere two miles from my neighborhood. Sociologists often attribute its success at racial integration to the fact that its residents—black and white—share a great deal of class cohesiveness. Its residents tend to be middle-class professionals with comfortable incomes. The economic and educational legacies of racism, however, do not create many such neighborhoods. Despite what Americans may believe, social class always has been and remains a powerful social marker in the culture. Undoubtedly, class is more fluid than race in some societies, but the invisible machine is always at work sorting, dividing, and diverting.

That ongoing sorting has been vastly aided by two inventions in the twentieth century. The automobile and television have dramatically altered the shape of human social life. The automobile became a powerful social architect of race and class. Highways and the personal, private, and insulating automobile allowed us to create environments defined by similar people and similar incomes. Wealthy neighborhoods (and the commercial centers and schools that accompany them) could—and did—move farther away from poor and struggling ones.

Jobs could move; people would commute. A new level of social isolation and stratification by class and income became possible.

Television began a process of drawing people indoors to the life of the screen. As screen technologies became more complex, people could construct virtual communities of their choice via the Internet and the blogosphere. Eventually, this led to the present age in which people in more affluent cultures can use screen tools to customize their entire view and experience of the world. Should we First-Worlders so choose, the Internet allows us to do what the automobile and cheap gas first made possible in new ways—to find and relate primarily to people we select. We can be in constant, instantaneous contact with those who share our interests and worldview. These two technologies fundamental to the twentieth century have made it possible to segregate by interest, income, race, and class in even more destructively stratified ways.

Annette Lareau, author of *Unequal Childhoods,* researched the effect of class background on parenting style. She observed families long-term, watching social interactions at home and at school. She found that class background created some common approaches across individual differences. In other words, a person's class also tended to determine certain gifts and deficits in that person's parenting.[1]

One of the primary markers of class difference was the use of language and vocabulary. Middle-class homes contain much more conversation. Parents talk conversationally with their children as a matter of course about a range of topics. Because verbal skill figures keenly in most of their professional lives, conversation naturally spills into family life. As a result, Lareau conjectures that the children of middle-class parents grow up to become stronger advocates for themselves, more comfortable around authority figures, and more able to negotiate verbally. These verbal skills give them an edge on the educational ladder, in the job market, and in their social lives.

My friend Maddie refers to "class attacks." She is an articulate, skilled, and professional woman. She could sell you the Golden Gate Bridge. She makes every person she meets feel like the wisest and funniest person on earth. Her eyes, hands, and face express poetry and conviction. I think, *Nothing can stop this woman.* But she finds herself less confident in speaking with a bank manager about her account. She explains, "I grew up in a working-class family and at an Irish-Catholic school where every classroom had more than fifty kids. In that situation, everything you are taught is about control. Teaching control uses two primary mechanisms. One is shame. The other is silence. To compound it all, everything at home was about how to feed and clothe nine kids on one working-class salary. Kids were never allowed to engage—much less question—adults. You were told what to do and when to do it and to be quiet.

"I wasn't raised to go into the office of a bank manager and say I have a problem with the bank's handling of my account. I was raised that I wasn't to speak out or disagree with authority figures, and I still have the sweats and shakes as I think of doing it. I have to take a friend with me. At critical moments, the friend has to jump in with her assertive and verbal middle-class self and make my case for me."

I don't understand all the complex manifestations of race and class that sometimes impinge on my relationships, but I know this: These manifestations run at subterranean and foundational levels, and they will rise at the most unexpected of times and interactions. Unless we choose some specifically class-defecting behavior—a very different kind of profession from our peers and parents or a completely different neighborhood demographic—we will be surrounded with folks like us. The largest differences that we might negotiate will be unusual personality quirks and habits.

Of course, the usual motivation for any class-defecting behaviors is to climb the social ladder, not to build a world that embodies more justice or social equality. The working-class woman who does well tries to ensure the networking and social possibilities of her children by investing in the best schools she can afford. Although sociologists tell us that a true migration from one class background into another social class normally "takes" only after three generations, superficial class movement occurs constantly. That superficial shifting explains why our culture lives under the illusion of being classless.

Yet, looking out my front window, I live with no illusions of living in a world of classlessness or of a world without race. That dream of a world in which race has no power seems like a dream I will not see incarnated in my lifetime. A racially neutral or classless society seems impossible.

After decades of unconventional choices I still must sit with the fact that most of my closest friendship are not as racially diverse as I wish. I am trying to change this, but the change is slow. Each hard-won relationship helps me see more clearly. When my innate racist assumptions reveal themselves, I have received unexpected and extraordinary grace from the friends whose lives have been most affected by the cultural legacy of racism.

In the Gospel of Mark, a blind man approaches Jesus to receive his sight. Jesus places his hands on the man's eyes and then asks him what he sees. "I see men, for I see them like trees, walking around" (Mark 8:24). The man's vision is better, but he still doesn't see. Jesus touches him again. Only then does he see clearly. I love that partial healing, the gentle sense that healing is a process and not a sudden miracle.

Author Sandra Tsing Loh describes the daily proces of working toward racial healing. "True integration, I think, does not result from a single grand dramtic gesture . . . . True integration evolves from daily, tiny, bridging human moments."[2] I resonate with the truth that in our racially scarred and segregated culture, each day presents us with many moments to heal the wounds of racism. Healing my racially conditioned eyes will take many touches. I know that now. But if I am persistent, I will come to see more clearly. That is my dream and my promise.

Chapter 16

Raising Children Across the Divide

Confessions on Race and Class II

My confrontation with race and class dynamics as I made alternative choices about my own neighborhoods and workplaces was relatively tame. To confront the real face of class and race dynamics in the United States, I had to raise children.

The world was pretty nonchalant about unconventional choices I made for myself. Choosing to live in a not-great neighborhood out of belief that I could be part of making it better? Okay. Forgoing nice things for myself so that I could siphon income over to people who struggle to pay for food and a roof and health care? Sure. Biking instead of driving a car and trying to raise my own food? Whatever. People were puzzled by my decisions but nonchalant. But when my unconventional lifestyle choices impacted my children, people got upset with me.

Starting with the birth experience onward, I noticed the quiet, intractable ways that race, class, and political paradigm affected my every parenting choice. While individual preferences influenced some decisions, many were determined by economics, income, access to health care, and social network.

At the root of such a range of choices lie our fears as parents and our fierce desire to protect our children. They represent the fundamental instincts of any parent—instincts as primal as love. We fear for our children in ways we do not fear for ourselves or other adults. In a world in which there is so much from which we can't protect them, why risk those things we do not have to risk?

Will and I were able to postpone many choices when our children were young and at home. But as they got older, the realities of the social structure beyond our household hit, and we confronted the polarization of choice—the options that middle-class, two-income salaries make possible versus the "public" options (where "public" has increasingly become synonymous with poor).

Will and I did not live in a neighborhood of kids with whom ours could easily play without negotiating some barriers. We didn't really know the parents of the children in our neighborhood (most were fifteen years younger), and those parents didn't know us. The race and class differences around how to raise children seemed, if not insurmountable, certainly daunting. I was trying to protect my kids from sugar and screens and guns and consumerism. Other mothers in my neighborhood were raising their kids indoors because it was safer there, so TV and computer games were good. Our instincts for disciplining our kids were different. So was almost everything else. Meeting other parents on the playground only panned out a few times. For the most part, parents didn't take their kids to the playground in our neighborhood. Children went accompanied by older siblings.

I have always quietly steered away from those (compelling) liberal education models—the Waldorf, Montessori, and Quaker schools with their trendy, alternative pedagogies—even though I love and embrace some of those approaches. I have done this simply on the basis that tuition costs for those schools are significant, which makes them less economically diverse. I am committed to a public education system, meaning my children attend public schools. (I've kept these convictions although I spent my last ten years of school in private institutions, an irony that does not escape me.)

I rage at a system that makes us choose between raising our children well and raising all children well. People say, "Don't sacrifice your kids." Yet kids are being sacrificed every day. Why should my child not face some small sacrifice as well? If there is any bone I pick with God, it is that the world is set up to favor those with money. I already have more privilege than 90 percent of the world so I can ensure that it is not my children who are sacrificed.

Sometimes I act as if my children are extensions of myself. Since I have already worked through denying myself certain things because of the privilege or consumerism they represent, why not deny my children these things as well? Yet, in reality, I am talking about my son, Luke, and my daughter, Thea. I am not my children. They contain their own complex personalities, weaknesses, triggers, and vulnerabilities, mysterious yet familiar. My friend Judith's opinion on the matter is clear: "I would never sacrifice my children. You have to go with your gut."

I find myself less decisive. If more parents put their children's lives and welfare in the same camp as the children who are poorest and need the most, what is available to all children would be better. If we all committed to education systems that took all children, regardless of class and wealth, we would have a better system.

I will never live in any true solidarity with the poor. But I do believe in the possibility and grace to learn from others about the silent, unjust, and usually misunderstood struggles many people on the margins experience. I hope to become wiser and therefore to be more able to participate in a divestment of power and privilege that may make the world more equal and less lopsided with status.

From choosing my children's school on, I constantly faced a polarization of choice and never found middle ground. Will and I could send our kids to the public pools at community recreation centers. There would be no clean (and sometimes no working) bathrooms and showers, no benches and chairs by the pool. There would be mobs of kids, and we were lucky to get a square foot of swimming space. Or we could spend a cool $700 and join a swim club that had beautiful lawns, chairs, and friends whom we knew and a social network we fit into easily.

Summer camps were either mostly white or mostly black. At the mostly white camps, icebreakers for the young campers included the economically revealing question, such as "How many countries have you visited?" and fees were upward of $250 per week for a day camp. The mostly black camps, staffed by bored teenagers, cost $80 per week or less, and maybe a handful of the kids had been outside the city.

I almost never found the middle ground—experiences that would not infect my children with a sense of privilege and entitlement but instead would give them a sense of the diversity and inequity in the world. I wanted my children to move through the world able to relate to and understand a variety of people. Yet I'm always forced to choose one extreme or the other. (One definition of privilege is that I get to choose.) Sometimes my kids are the only white kids. Sometimes all the kids—or the vast majority—are white or middle class.

Each environment carries a different risk. When my children are "only," they experience the dangerous pressure of serving as the example of an entire group. In such contexts, even as a grown woman, I worry about whether I will stand out, so I can imagine the impact of this situation on my children. If they misbehave, will that become a verdict for all white children? Will they really be treated as peers, or will the other kids keep them at a distance?

Yet white environments scare me more, first with all the privileges they quietly pass along and also because of the cancer of racism they can spread. The first time that I ever heard my son use the phrase "black kids"—and use it disparagingly—was two days into a summer recreation camp in an affluent part of town that was 65 percent white. He was almost five years old. If he'd been in his usual settings, where he was a racial minority, he would not have picked up that phrase. He heard older kids talking and making distinctions about race that would not have occurred to him. Yet once suggested, they were not easy to erase. He was given the primitive categories of race into which we cram everything. He had caught the disease.

Before that moment, it was clear that my son noticed that he was different from his classmates, and he sometimes explored these differences with childish assertions, trying to figure out the mired and distorted legacy of race in America. He'd tell me that his friend Henry's family came from Africa, and I would tell him about the continents and countries that our family came from as well. Most of his friends were not white. As he tried to understand his environment, he told me, "Mommy, some people are white, and some people are black."

I honored his struggle of differentiation, but I feared the power race consciousness brings. I understand how God felt in Eden when the created children start eating from the tree of knowledge of good and evil. Unpacking that knowledge is a necessity, but it is terrifying. I did not know how it would shape his consciousness.

So I responded, "But the colors really don't matter. I'm not really white; others are not really black. Skin comes in many shades. We just *call* people yellow, black, red, and white."

"Yeah! Yes!" he replied with his characteristic enthusiasm for joining the conversation. Then he confides again that insight he has offered before. "Well, mostly there are black people in the world, but there are *some* whites."

That was his reality—his neighborhood, his school, his church.

I would like to believe that my children will grow up more bicultural than I, with more authentic relationships across boundaries of race, class, and experience. I hope that I can offer them the gift of growing up in a world where many kinds of discrimination have finally lost their power. This seems such a beautiful and critical offering for the healing of the world. It would not be my choice for them to be the extreme minority in so many settings, but it is their reality right now. I am not sure how this gift will work out. But I want the best for them—especially that they grow up in an America that is more racially healed. I look at the young African-American boys and girls who are my children's friends, and I want desperately for them to keep their self-love intact in a world poised to destroy it. I want us all to be saved.

A few years ago, I took my son, then six years old, to a local screening of *Standing On My Sisters' Shoulders,* a documentary about the women of Mississippi in the civil rights movement. Though I found the film to be courageous and moving in its own right, I was most captivated by my first-grade son's response. He was riveted by the stories and images of a world before integration—a world he only had heard and read about. This film was his first time to see footage, some of it harsh, of sit-ins and marches and to listen to accounts by the women who waged a transformative battle in what was arguably the most violent and intractable frontier of the movement.

In the film, Mae Bertha Carter, sharecropper and mother of thirteen, tells the story of integrating her county's schools. As she relayed the threats and hostility her children endured in a voice-over, the camera panned over school yearbook pages with the photos of her children, always the one somber black face in a sea of smiling white faces. I watched my son for some glimmer of recognition as he took in those yearbook spreads. The yearbook of his publicly funded school that year showed twenty-seven smiling faces in his class. His was the only fair-skinned, blue-eyed face.

I try not to engage in discouraging thoughts. The civil rights movement did not fail, and it is not a lie when I tell my son that people of all races have much more opportunity because of the amazing courage and faith of these women and men. Yet, the reality is that only a few middle-class white couples from my fairly wide circle of white friends are committed to using the public school system for their children. All the other middle-class couples I know have quietly chosen other options. The massive desertion of the urban public school systems by middle-class whites in my city is startling. Most disheartening is that these are white people who understand how our world has been reshaped by racism.

When Will and I decided to send our children to public schools, we had moral grounding for our choice. We both believed that accessible and good education is the basis of a democracy and a more just society. If we advocated for and wanted a broad-based public education, we felt we should be prepared to use that system for our own children. But when it comes to white professionals making choices about the schooling of their own kids, I've learned that—as a group—we are much more comfortable raising our middle-class kids in small, mostly white private schools and teaching them to change the world (and break down class and race barriers) as adults rather than actually trusting them to the public system for which we advocate—and in the process confronting those race and class barriers themselves.

My children's schools and the schools where my friends send their children may have little to do with Mississippi schools in the sixties, which operated under a legally enforced apartheid system. Yet, as education activist and teacher Johnathan Kozol points out, the school district in the South Bronx where he's spent most of the past fifteen years has eleven thousand students in elementary and middle schools. Twenty-six of these students are white. Kozol notes, "That's a segregation rate of 99.8 percent. Two-tenths of 1 percent mark the difference between legally enforced apartheid in Mississippi fifty years ago, and socially and economically enforced apartheid in New York today."[1] Considering that the civil rights movement—and the end of segregation—is arguably this nation's best story of nonviolent and democratic change, this is a tragic reality to pass on to our children.

Studies like "Race in American Schools: Rapidly Resegregating School Districts" from The Civil Rights Project of Harvard University show that in recent years US public schools in every region are resegregating. In the last ten years, as court orders for desegregation have been allowed to expire, the careful gains of racial balance won over the years have begun to erode. Although minority enrollment in US schools has reached almost 40 percent nationwide, the average white student still attends a public school that is 80 percent white. Meanwhile, in the Midwest and Northeast, where I live, more than a quarter of black students attend schools that are nearly 100 percent nonwhite. The Civil Rights Project report points out that between 1964 and 1988, the percentage of black students in the South who attended majority white schools rose from 2.3 percent to 43.5 percent, but that number declined 13 percentage points in the 1990s. In 2002, that percentage was at its lowest level since 1968.[2]

My children's school district spends $8,500 per student. If my family were to move two miles north to Cheltenham, the school district there would spend $13,227 per child. Beyond, in the wealthy county of Bucks, that figure jumps to $14,865. Johnathon Kozol notes that in the New York suburbs, the public spends $12,000 a year per student in Roosevelt, Long Island, which is 92 percent poor. In the neighboring city of Manhasset (5 percent poor), the district spends $22,000 per student.[3] I remain angry and puzzled about the "unsolvable" issues of public education. It seems to me that a nation that houses some of the most advanced technology in the world is capable of creating a public education system that spends an equal amount on every child. If equitable funding is impossible, the vision of a truly just educational system becomes even more elusive.

I don't know whether the system is kept in place by the intentional desire to create an underclass, as some argue. Many of us do not like the system, and yet we hardly know how to counteract the monster. It is much easier, if we have the resources, to withdraw to the well-funded suburb, or to adhere to our creative curricula, small, private schools, or homeschool models. The public school system is deeply flawed—an easy target for criticism on every side. Yet few of the white parents whom I know have observed a single public classroom before deciding against it.

I spend my time at and pour my resources into the schools that my kids attend. My friends do the same. I would be deluding myself to think that parents of children in fully-resourced schools would have the time and energy to fight for better schools for those "other" kids. Yet if those of us who do have resources, education, and commitment continue not to be engaged in the most struggling schools, they will not improve. Here is the question that faces socially conscious people: To what degree do we make unconventional and difficult social choices because they can lead toward the possibility of a more equitable vision for society?

Theologian Rodney Stark points out that the poverty, disease, and social chaos in Antioch (the Roman city that gave rise to the Gospel of Matthew) ultimately gave the Christian witness its power. In the midst of deplorable conditions, Christianity offered a vital alternative. In a city with a population density greater than Bombay, with poor sanitation and open sewers, endless plagues and epidemics, the Christian community cared for its sick members and nursed them back to health. In a region of many cultural clashes and where families were broken apart, the church was a place where very different people found kinship and community. At a time when the gap between rich and poor was growing, Christianity preached that everyone was equal in the eyes of God.[4] These were seeds of revolution.

I am taken by a vision of a community that shows people how to live humanely in places of chaos, disaffection, and poverty. I dream of being part of a spiritual community that sees its existence as a radical challenge to social divisions—a community willing to displace itself in order to engage in the difficult work of understanding new ways to build relationships of love. I wonder if such a community will dare risk not only its own security but also that of its children.

My father stands across from me in the kitchen of his beach house. Will, the children, and I are visiting on a family vacation, a spot on this earth we love. When we walk to the end of the beach, it seems like we are at the edge of the wild, beautiful world.

My children have gone to bed, and my father clearly wants to talk about something that has been weighing on him heavily. But when he broaches the topic, I am unprepared. He wants to know why I would do this to my children—send them to public schools in the city, live in my neighborhood.

"Think about your life. Your mother and I sent you to schools with kids like you, and the best schools we could afford. Would you rather have had a life like you had—or a life like your daughter's? Are you making your children an ideological experiment?"

I see he is in agony over what he perceives their lives to be. I know that he is asking out of love and deep fear for them. I am afraid also, unsure where this path Will and I have chosen will take my children or me. Every path has wounds, and we cannot choose which ones we will carry. But I want him to see their school—lovely and bright the hallways, teachers who really care, kids who care about my children. I want him to know that my children spend every afternoon playing outside as I did. Though we may live in the city, we hike and ride bikes and have friends over. I want him to see how the teenagers in our African American church in the heart of the most depressed part of the city take care of my kids and delight in them. I want him to see the gatherings of friends at our house—how finally blended and easy all the races and cultures are. I want him at the arts festival at Will's workplace, a nonprofit committed to fair housing. The festival features an open mike; while artists paint at a back table, my daughter belts out sultry blues songs and brings down the house. I want him to see my son, only eight, courageously stand up at a rally of four hundred and tell all the kids they need to fight for civil rights like Martin Luther King Jr. did.

I think we are okay.

"This life," I whisper, "has its own richness because it is sustainable. It doesn't depend on having a lot of money. It is not rooted in elitist and stratified social choices. It isn't built on segregating people like us and those who are different. I think, Daddy, that this is the path to a less frightening world. This is the way to a world less afraid of the future."

Isn't all of parenting an experiment? Should we not try some experiments that embody our truest hopes?

Chapter 17

This Reeling Earth

Confessions of a First-World Consumer I

Growing up with acres of land outside my door, I spent long afternoons and evenings wandering the woods and overgrown pasture. They were my deepest source of solitude and my place of prayer. They were my friend in the way no person will ever be. I was never lonely, though I was often alone. The natural world reminded me that I was one stitch in a huge, intricate pattern. It whispered to me of possibility, beauty, and mortality all at once.

To say my life and spiritual health depend on the rhythms of the natural world sounds almost foolish. After all, whose life does not? Yet my spiritual grounding depends on significant, daily contact with the earth, its trees, and its creature life. This is true even though I have lived in dense, urban areas all of my adult life—a feat that I could never have accomplished without a community garden plot and my current, quirky housing arrangement that, though smack in the middle of a low-income urban neighborhood, has lots of green.

This intense connection to earth means that I am haunted by the environmental plight of our planet. All my life, I have watched sprawl and development devour landscapes I've loved. I've watched species disappear and observed most of us buy bottled water as if it were normal—no outcry at a water system that can no longer be trusted to be safe. I have lived by taking more than my share of this world's resources. And I probably will betray my brothers and sisters on this planet by continuing to do so for the rest of my life. I am a First-World person, and that is a hard addiction from which to recover.

When Guan Ayi, my host for many months in China, came to live in the United States with me three years after my time in her country, I was confronted with all the ways I undermined her life of small economies. I had already slipped back into the currents of US consumption.

Shortly after her arrival in the country, I took Guan Ayi to the local library. I left her by the copy machine while I tracked down a book. When I came back, she was stuffing an inch-thick wad of white paper into her tiny bag. She turned to me and remarked incredulously, "Someone threw this away!" After two months in the United States, she was still shocked by the constant waste. In her homeland, wood was rare and precious. The fine white paper went home with us. The next morning, she was up early, industriously folding, cutting, and shaping the paper into beautifully symmetrical envelopes. "I'm running out of envelopes," she explained. I didn't tell her that I salvage at least six envelopes a day from junk mail or that thirty envelopes cost one dollar at Walgreens. Instead, I loaned her a glue stick.

That night, a pile of immaculate envelopes lay glued and stacked on her table. "I didn't use your glue," she said, returning it. "It's expensive. I used the starch from leftover breakfast noodles that stuck to the bottom of the pot. Otherwise they would have been wasted."

The gulf between our experiences yawned as wide as the thirteen thousand miles between our homelands. I was acutely conscious that three-quarters of the world shared her understanding of scarcity and make-do-ness, the preciousness and the vast art of conserving resources. It was painful for her to witness my First-World waste. What kind of spiritual stretching must I do to understand the way her experiences of scarcity have shaped her? How will she understand me?

Possessions—what we have, what we share, and what we are willing to live without—are a spiritual issue. They can help others, but they can also weigh us down. Protecting our lifestyle has been a seed of the wars in the past five decades. Our possessions impede our ability to relate to or even understand the human experience in most of the (poorer) parts of the world.

I recall the story of Jesus' conversation with the rich young ruler. Jesus says to him, "If you wish to enter into life, keep the commandments" (Matt. 19:17). The young man tells Jesus that he is already keeping the commandments, and he asks what else he should do. Jesus responds, "If you wish to be complete, go and sell your possessions and give to the poor" (Matt. 19:21). But Jesus does not stop there. He continues, "Come, follow Me" (Matt. 19:21). The young man leaves in grief, knowing that he has many possessions.

More and more, I suspect that if we ever came to take that story seriously, we'd all be learning how to reorient our lives. Maybe even how to make our own envelopes.

As I have gotten older, I find myself weighed down by the energy needed to resist the seductions of our throwaway culture. Not to gather stuff in a society full of stuff takes constant vigilance. We don't even have to *buy* stuff to acquire it. In our whacked-out society, it is possible to live well on what other people throw away. When my husband and I trash-picked our washing machine off the curb, it was in perfect working order. Fifteen years later, it has never needed a repair. Some of the people I know with the most stuff are those who simply keep what others are throwing out. I share that same instinct of saving useful things that others deem trash. But I can clutter my life with all that saving!

I track our family budget. We "need" more than we used to, but that need is also an illusion and a choice. Most of the items on that list move far beyond our needs for basic survival to include fun activities, small gadgets, and little luxuries. Like most Americans, we have a large carbon footprint. (Here in the United States, we have only 4 percent of the world's population, but we produce 25 percent of its greenhouse gases.)

Occasionally I visit friends who live by a vow of poverty, such as my hermit monk friend Richard. Richard inspires my children with stories of how he bought his row home for a dollar from the city at a sheriff's sale. Unable to conceive of the expense and years it took him to install electricity, plumbing, walls, windows, they think this is cool. After all, they have one dollar! When I return from Richard's, I reflect on how he has stayed faithful to that vow of poverty while I am living the shadow of that middle-class life, everything I need and more. I feel sullied somehow. I want to be reconciled to my younger self, to Guan Ayi, to Richard.

A few years back, my family considered moving to a rural community and living in a small, off-the-grid house on a patch of not-rich-but-adequate land. We wanted a life of simplicity and hospitality—growing most of our food instead of a tenth of it, living two steps further outside the cash economy. We dreamed of a life of resistance and defection from the culture.

Most of the lifestyles I admire I've also romanticized. An ocean of moral compromises exists in my world. Everywhere I turn, I see something worth resisting. But living out consistent cultural opposition on a couple of fronts (one cannot do them all) while the broader culture thinks I am a loony takes energy. It is much easier to live on less in a society where everyone else also participates in those economies. But easy or hard, I see no alternative. Once I seriously began to confront issues of poverty and justice, I had no spiritual or ethical alternative but to change my pattern of living radically—what I ate, what I bought, my modes of travel, and where I lived.

We live in a season of injustice. Never before has a people's ordinary, unquestioning participation in established social and economic structures ushered in such large-scale exploitation, disparity of wealth and power, and ecological destruction. Merely to live within our current economic system requires collusion in structures that are destroying our ecosystem as well as human community.

Many of us want to live in gentle, healing ways toward one another and the earth, but we find this excruciatingly difficult to do. Do we buy food that is ethically produced or food that fits our (self-styled, subsistence) food budget? We can barely find jobs, much less jobs not founded on materialism, the hierarchy of education and class, the unbalanced workaholism, and the crazy commute that are hallmarks of our age. While we know that constant use of cars is destroying the ozone layer, structuring a life without one is anything but simple living. So many factors play into my daily choices that the smallest purchase creates endless questions. *Do I need it? Who had been harmed in its production, and upon whom are its real cost being off-loaded?*

For many years, my attempts at living more simply caught me in a wave of painful emotions—guilt, stress (created by choosing time-consuming methods of doing things without freeing up ways to have more time), and feelings of judgment toward others (I was secretly angry that they were not making the same choices because that made it harder for me to keep to my choices). I fought internal voices calling me too indulgent and rebel voices calling me too ascetic. Not to mention the friends and family who found me extreme.

Only now, after years of working through these issues, does the root problem penetrate my consciousness. My external changes had far outpaced my internal transformation. I had not acknowledged how deeply my interior life had been co-opted and colonized by the external systems into which I was socialized. On the surface, I was living out a different set of choices, but internally I was not. I was competitive. I was righteous about my "deprivations." (I felt they were deprivations precisely because I still wanted some of those things. But I didn't allow myself to have them because I was too conscious of the unjust systems behind them.) The negative emotions that fueled the economic chaos and rat race around me were rooted in me just as deeply. I was fundamentally discontent.

How do we discuss *simple living* in a time of political polarization and economic collapse? Even the phrase comes loaded with images of narrow, stubborn reactionaries who refuse to adapt to a changing world. The idea of simple living reeks of choosing a life of long, grim Lenten practices in which every indulgence (a vacation, chocolate, a movie) is met with soul-searching guilt. No, it has to be different.

Our lives and imaginations are not fed by opposition. A fresh vision can carry us toward the life-giving waters for which we truly yearn. How do we root ourselves not in opposition but in forward-leaning, expectant imagination?

I see two different ways of living out an opposition to globalization, consumerism, and exploitation. We can spend our lives in direct confrontation with those forces. Or we can live in a way that creates a new alternative that carries us toward a different, more life-giving destination so that the destructive way of life is no longer compelling. Often we begin rooted in the energy of opposition with the conviction of fighting something. Yet if we continue, we ultimately pick up and leave that war. We begin to shape lives over which the forces we are fighting have less power. The war itself becomes irrelevant. We find a path that takes away the power of the evil.

Members of the early church were called "followers of the Way." They were led by the Spirit to shape a new path. Although that path led them in direct opposition to established temple religion (of both the Jewish priests and of Rome) and into the teeth of the Empire, fighting the religious powers or the empire was not their rallying cry. The early Christian community drew people irresistibly because it offered a rich alternative. New followers were enveloped into a family of faith that offered care and support. Early Christianity grew because people prayed together, read the Word together, and looked after one another's basic needs for food or shelter. Historians tell us that Christians nursed each other through the plagues of fatal illness that rampaged through the densely populated, unsanitary Roman cities, while other groups abandoned the ill to their death. In its origins, if not now, the Christian community offered relationship, care, and survival in harsh times.

In the biography *Harlan Hubbard: Life and Work*, author Wendell Berry tells the remarkable story of Anna and Harlan Hubbard. Together Anna and Harlan lived out a forty-year Walden Pond experience on the banks of the Ohio River—a rich life of sustenance on the land, reading, music, art, and occasional forays into civilization to take in a concert or two. (As Harlan once commented, "What manner of a man originated this idea of a happier life beyond death?"[1])

In their later years, Harlan and Anna lived off the land against the backdrop of a local, grassroots campaign fighting the expansion of a local power plant. Berry notes that Harlan and Anna did not participate in a local demonstration against a power plant, a decision many neighbors and other folk did not understand. Berry drew the following conclusion:

> Later, I understood that by the life they led Harlan and Anna had opposed the power plant longer than any of us, and not because they had been or ever would be its "opponents." They were opposed to it because they were opposite to it, because their way of life joined them to everything in the world that was opposite to it. What could be more radically or effectively opposite to a power plant than to live abundantly with no need for electricity?[2]

I am not writing this book from that off-the-grid community house. There are many good reasons to be where I am, writing from the neighborhood I've been part of for more than twenty-five years. I know that I am complicit in using more than my share of earth's resources in making the choice to be here. But I am moving forward. In the words of Mary Oliver in her poem "John Chapman," I am "caring about something."[3]

Chapter 18

Who Will Save the Frogs?

Confessions of a First-World Consumer II

When it comes right down to it, I seem unable to address in any significant way the damage of the earth, the vast and mysterious creation I love more than anything or any being on it. The looming crisis of the earth haunts me. Every unseasonable stretch of days (heat, cold, excessive rain, violent winter and summer storms) serves as a reminder of the ways that human choices are contributing to changing the system that nurtures us. Our denial of our responsibility runs deep.

A few years back, I was scraping oatmeal into the compost bucket and listening to the radio when a BBC news trailer captured my full attention. In the five-second news clip, a scientist explained that a mysterious fungus was killing many species of frog worldwide. Frogs were at risk of sudden extinction. The thought was stunning and horrible.

Playing with Legos in the adjoining room sat my son, a boy passionate about frogs. From March well into November, my family spends countless afternoons and evenings around woods and ponds, listening to frogs' choruses swell and fade. We train our eyes to adjust to the subdued intricacies of nature's amazing camouflage until we can finally spot them in the grass, mud, and murky waters. Together, we have identified most of the species common to our region. I probably have fifty photographs of my son holding various species of frogs—his hands completely gentle and his face lit with a smile.

A sense of panic and foreboding rose in me, and I couldn't stop myself from running into the living room. "Luke! This news report says that frogs are becoming extinct—some fungus is killing them."

Among many moments of bad parenting, this instance ranks among the most ill thought out. My son fell prone on the sofa, buried his face in the pillow, and sobbed. His sister ran to him to see what he was crying about and to comfort him. He could not be comforted. He would not be torn from the pillow covered in his anguished tears. His shoulders heaved with silent sobs for a full three minutes before he lifted his contorted face. "Mommy," he whispered, "I cannot live without frogs."

His was a literal statement, of course. Without frogs, a critical link in the food chain would be broken. The "canary" of the water table, the one that warns us of environmental danger, would be absent. Like so many of the predictions around environmental impact, the aftermath of such a catastrophe is not completely foreseeable but would surely be dire. We must ask ourselves how dire, how soon, and what might be reparable at this late hour?

And yet my son's was also a spiritual statement. My children felt an empathy for this planet that they cannot put into words—an empathy that persuaded them to become vegetarians at the age of five and seven because they could no longer bear to eat a creature that had been killed for the express purpose of feeding them. The thought of living in a world without frogs, one of the creatures my son adored and watched constantly, was unfathomable to him.

I grapple with how to prepare my children for a future in which the foundation of life as we know it—this planet herself—promises to be in dramatic shift. Human actions will make it impossible to reverse some of that shift. The certainties that have marked my life—seasons, plant and animal life forms, landscapes on this earth—will become altered in my son's life, perhaps beyond recognition. Already a feeling of loss comes over me when my husband describes the winters of his Midwestern childhood—skating on the frozen rivers, playing on ice mountains that thawed only in April and not before. In his lifetime, fifty years, this experience is, quite simply, gone.

We can win some battles. Our moral courage—our ability to forgo money, power, or comfort for what is better and more beautiful for the common good—may be what will win them. That morning, staring into my son's anguished eyes, I felt my helplessness arise again in a new way. Our children will inherit this planet, but they have little control about how their parents live, consume energy, and teach the next generation. We are failing them by raising them in an artificial and unsustainable world of comfort uncritical of materialism and disposability. Yet, our children are the ones who will taste the bitter fruit of our inability to deny ourselves convenience and ease. Our failed leadership in this planetary crisis threatens to destroy something significant in their lives.

Understandably, attempting to live sustainably on this earth became a passion in my life. For a host of reasons, I have tried to live frugally. I want to tread lightly on a planet that I find to be very polluted and endangered. I want to live with my hands—not just my head—so I have tried to learn basic life skills that many of my generation have never learned, such as growing and putting up a good amount of my own food and learning to make basic home repairs. I want to step out of unjust production systems that are the hallmark of our era, and I mostly do that by trying not to buy much at all and by recycling as much trash as I can. (A woman in Seattle who produces two trash cans of refuse a year serves as my inspiration.)

A "green" way of life is available to folks with a certain level of disposable income—organic grocery stores, ecologically sensitive cleaning products, electric or hybrid cars, energy-saving dishwashers and washing machines, and a host of earth-friendly accent items advertised in magazines. My own low-tech "green" life is full of secondhand equipment that breaks down, never-ending chores, and ongoing moral dilemmas about wants and needs. This life demands time I do not have. A friend tells me I would be a much better advocate for sustainable living if I did a bit less from scratch, used a few more labor-saving devices, and put the time I saved into clear, focused advocacy for ecological policies. She is probably right.

I am aware of the tremendous contradictions embedded in the choices I make—when I drive a car to a demonstration against drilling for oil in the Arctic, for example. When I lead workshops on the freedom of simplicity, I often want to begin with the confession that "simple living" is, at one level, a big complication. The three Rs—reduce, reuse, and recycle—aren't glamorous. They are gritty, inconvenient, and time-consuming.

How can I, as a parent, prepare my children for a time of severe environmental shift while trapped in a way of living that perpetuates environmental loss and damage? I am reminded of the apocryphal story of Mahatma Gandhi and the sugar lesson. A worried mother drags her child over many miles to Gandhi, and she asks him to admonish the child not to eat sugar because of its ill effects on his health. Gandhi asks her to return home with her son and to come back in two weeks. Upon her return, Gandhi looks at the child and admonishes him, "Don't eat sugar."

"Why couldn't you just tell him that two weeks ago!" the mother grouses. "Why did I have to come back?"

Gandhi replies, "Because two weeks ago, I had not yet given up sugar."

Essentially we face a similar dilemma. We are addicted to a disposable and emission-dependent way of living. My generation is deeply compromised and implicated in energy-hogging lifestyles. Our solutions to climate change and the inevitable extinction of oil have a certain predictability. We are waiting for the silver bullet—the clean alternative fuel that will allow us to keep running all our gadgets, only running them cleaner. We believe in and seek the miracle that will allow us to keep our lives the same.

Too few of us are willing to do without. The fact is, I *could* actually give up our car. My family lives in a major urban area. A basic, if sometimes clunky, public transportation system exists. I lived without a car for a decade before kids. But in reality, though I am intentional about biking more and driving less and I try to structure my family's life in ways that are less car-dependent, actually getting rid of the car is a huge task. With four people in my family, not all of whom are bikers yet, this would be a more drastic step than I wish to take. So I make relatively benign changes to my life—I use energy-efficient light bulbs, recycle, carpool, grow food, and compost. But fundamentally I continue to participate in the world of production and consumption because of the difficulty of stepping out of it, even though it is not sustainable and exists—and perhaps depends on—others elsewhere staying poor. I am holding back. *What am I waiting for?* I ask myself. For that great Parent in the sky to hand down a governmental edict and *make* me do what I am capable of choosing now?

As I held my devastated, weeping son in the wake of the prediction about frogs, I fiercely believed I would do anything to change the direction of the world, to save the frogs, to lessen the deep scar of the human footprint on the planet. In a rush of empathy, I envisioned embracing vegetarianism and never giving a second glance at bacon.

When the full BBC story came on later, I was finally wise enough to listen apart from my son, and I passed on the hopeful parts to him. Biologists and other preservationists are keeping special, fungus-free colonies of frogs and breeding them until the fungus can be addressed. The fungus isn't caused by climate change. (This latter assertion was quickly overturned, as scientists showed that the fungus is spreading because of an incremental increase in temperature.)

After my briefing, my son and daughter gathered around the kitchen table and conspired. They discussed their $50 in Christmas money from grandparents, still untouched. The day before, they had decreed that $5 would be going to the homeless and the rest to some yearned-for toys, but that day, they felt that they could give half to protect the frogs. I loved their spirit: "If we give $25, that is quite a lot," said my son. "That will really help. They can buy three heat lamps for the frogs with that."

In their naïveté, my son and daughter are more effective than I. Every day, I feel the world collapsing around me. Warm days in January make me tense. I ponder environmental chaos and crisis and the immensity of the conversion from an oil economy and become overwhelmed. (Being overwhelmed is directly connected to feeling powerless.) I am not as hopeful as my children are.

As parents, we always stumble on that moment that we love and hate when we suddenly realize the shoe is on the other foot. Our children are reshaping us in necessary but wrenching ways—ways that will make us better human beings. My children do not feel powerless. Hope is one gift of youth—there is always time; there is always the possibility of change; there is always grace. I want them to take me where I have not myself dared to go.

In return, what do I give to my children? I teach them to notice the world. I help them learn to call each flower, tree, and animal by name. I teach them to appreciate this place that holds us as we walk through our days in an urban neighborhood. We do those small, intentional things that become habit—gardening, composting, recycling, biking, riding the city bus, getting rid of the dryer so we *have* to use a clothesline, living in a house that is small by US standards, keeping our heat low in winter, and living with fans and no air conditioning in the summer. We talk constantly about the difference between needs and wants and how we can find freedom from those wants. We talk about who is making our clothes and shoes and where the trash goes.

In my battered file cabinet resides a stack of yellow, crumbled letters written between my maternal great-grandparents, Rufus and Ella, and Rufus's sister, Leila. These letters are more than one hundred years old. He was a schoolteacher and principal in Georgia. Leila, his unmarried sister, lived on the old homestead with her parents in Prosperity, South Carolina, where there was nothing prosperous about the hardscrabble red land. Their small up-country farm grew vegetables and cotton.

Rufus had found his niche in his local schoolhouse—he was a gifted, formidable, and respected teacher. Yet, despite the fact that his vocations were teacher, principal, and ultimately superintendent of a school district, these letters are full of his home economies—his garden and peach patches, his cotton, and how many hogs he slaughtered in the fall. This news—coupled with who was sick and who was well and sundry family details—make up the quiet conversation in the letters, the only day-to-day glimpse I have of his life.

In that era, most people had some sort of relationship to the land. People grew much of their own food and kept livestock for their meat. Of course, many made their living from the land. But what intrigues me is that no one seemed to live independently of it. Even respected, white-collar professionals in the community knew the craft and necessity of living off the land. No one's vegetables were trucked in from California or flown in from Chile. People needed land to live in the most elemental way. We no longer grasp this reality. My grandfather's letters remind me of all the knowledge that we have lost.

My daughter has stayed on my case to become vegetarian, a choice she made at six. With the zeal only the converted know, she has pressed me to do the same. I know that she stands on moral ground. Most people are probably omnivores for no greater reason than they like eating meat and don't want to give that up. I certainly am.

"Mommy, why do people even eat animals? We have so much food without eating animals—too much food. We have so much food we are fat. We have food like chips! Why eat an animal?" She falls silent. Then she continues. "I just keep imagining myself as an animal in this world—a fish, a bird, a small squirrel living in my little beautiful home. And then *bam*—just like that, I'm dead. I lose my whole life because someone else is hungry for me!"

Because I love her and know that her argument carries moral weight, this past Lent I slid into my meat abstinence—a week after Ash Wednesday. My daughter proposed a strategy to help me. "Here's what you do, Mommy. Every time you see a piece of meat, you imagine it in its lovely life—what a beautiful animal it was on this earth, how it looked. Then you look at the meat and think how ugly it is, and you won't want to eat it."

I want to be intentional and consistent, yet I am not. Walt Whitman offers these insightful (and often liberating) words in his poem "Song of Myself": "Do I contradict myself? / Very well then I contradict myself, / (I am large; I contain multitudes.)" While reassuring, Whitman gives us wisdom and a convenient justification for hypocrisy. In those moments when we give ourselves a break—allowing ourselves to partake of an indulgence—we may sense a loss and a grief of not being who we yearn to be. My commitment to live sustainably (which could be defined as purchasing and eating all organic food grown within one hundred miles of my home) is at war with my commitment to live on little money.

Our deepest dreams often war with one another. For instance, my workplace at *The Other Side* limited salaries, keeping them at about half the national median household income (which has hovered around $40–50K for decades). The magazine adopted this practice as a conscious, organizational statement, an attempt to define "enough" in a culture that thought nothing of consuming the vast majority of the world's resources. We were committed to living nonconsumptively as well as to having some reality check that kept us in touch with the struggles of truly low-income people. Very few organizations willingly take a courageous stand like that, yet the policy became a quiet barrier to employing those we most wanted at the table. Many people of color, immigrants, and first-generation college graduates needed or wanted market-rate compensation. Their families had sacrificed to educate them and expected them to do well and give generously to the family. Our desire to be conservative about resources and consumption effectively jeopardized attempts to employ those who were not middle-class, educated, and resourced. No matter how pure our vision and hope, we live in a constant state of wrenching compromise.

One of the most enigmatic yet hauntingly beautiful refrains of scripture is found in Psalm 137: "If I forget thee, O Jersalem, let my right hand forget her cunning" (v. 5, KJV). First penned in an economy fueled completely by manual work, this verse evokes the greatest, most devastating loss: a body losing its knowledge of survival skills and of how to live in the world, which created a path toward certain death.

Yet that word *cunning* is neither altogether pure nor lovely. Its meaning hints at shrewd intelligence and some self-preservation. A cunning person is smart, but he or she uses that gift to advance. Cunning is brilliance without altruism, the stone that shines but also cuts. Perhaps we need to lose the quality of being cunning—the sense that we know what will happen and what doors we are opening with our technologies and our comforts.

Can we turn back from and relinquish some inventions and conveniences for the sake of life? Rarely has this instinct in humans been tested. Can we forsake some invention or technological path we know is possible and alluring because it threatens to destroy us or others? Can we unlearn the habit of progress—that what can be done and imagined therefore must be tried? Or may we instead intentionally choose what we set aside as well as what we embrace? Are we willing to live differently and, by many people's definition, less well, so that the planet might be more whole? My son's tears over frogs are only a portent of a thousand lost and beautiful life forms to come; a planet turned off course.

Can our right hand lose its cunning?

My husband grew ill and spent a week in the hospital for the mind. The place he stayed has luscious grounds, one reason I could imagine him resting and recuperating. But once he was there, I discovered no patients were allowed to go outside. They could only look out at the greening spring.

The day I went to bring him home, I pondered all that we do not know about healing. My husband and I walked, hands clasped, joyful to be together, though he was shaken and tentative. How to bring this earth, also sad and reeling a bit, back to itself? I wrote a poem.

Release from the Ward

After days of trying locks,
the double set of hospital doors
opened onto the tulip magnolia,
twisted and weeping with purple joy, the gold, wild-eyed
    forsythia,
and the buttercups, nodding in silent understanding. We
    walked out,
hand in hand to the pond.
No frogs, turtles to be found.
Just yesterday flurries of snow floated icy petals
across its silence. An old willow at
the water's edge has genuflected one final time. The young
    boy clambers out on the trunk of it, above the
    precarious water
while his small sister sits securely astride the exposed roots,
riding toward whatever the future might hold—
fire this summer, she imagines.
(She knows the earth
is warming rapidly now.)
In her mind, everything will spontaneously combust—
her too—but now it is still the edge of spring,
so she clambers off the tree and wanders into the bamboo
    forest
delighting in this world.
She eats the first leaves of garlic mustard with relish,
telling us how much she will miss all this, the animals, us.
    And you, upon whom the dark angel sat these many
    days, you smile. It is possible to smile
though what she imagines will come to pass,
more or less. Already the bruised shadow
of evenfall haunts the treeline. When it all crumbles,
let me remember still
the tang of onion grass in my mouth;

how the light fell brilliant from the west;
how it slivered the bamboo grove into rods of gold.

On the way home, finally together as a family again, my son told me a new fairy tale. The threat to frogs is now many months behind us. Yet some memory lingered in him because his fairy tale included frogs disappearing from earth. Everyone assumed they were dying, he explained, and all the earth was in mourning. "But actually," continued Luke, "the frogs are leaving their homes on earth, which is getting darker and scarier, and going to their own paradise. They are finding their places and living. And in those new places, the frogs are the most beautiful colors, and they are singing new songs, every one."

I was not sure what to dream in return. The seasons folded over and turned, each carrying alarming aberrations mixed with all the beauty. We continued to live in uncertain and anxious times.

Like the woman, we go to the Holy One. "Come, you giver of gifts and dreams; you who have promised good things. Do not lie to us. Can you bring us back to life?"

PART IV

Finding Our Own Face

And [Elisha] went up and lay on the child, and put his mouth on
his mouth and his eyes on his eyes and his hands on his hands, and
he stretched himself on him; and the flesh of the child became warm.
2 Kings 4:34

Life is the slow discovery of who we are—especially our limits or the
places we stop.

To cherish—a slow, meditative form of love, relentless in its passion, persisting over time. Only if we cherish others will we ever
have the courage to know their true faces or to touch the shadows
in their souls.

And then, like a miracle, life is right there, just at skin level—hand
on hand, mouth on mouth—a breathing hope that refuses to let go,
a gratitude larger than any part of me.

Chapter 19

The Truth about Dreams

The ancient story unfolds in all its grief and loss. What can it teach me?

Then Gehazi passed on before them and laid the staff on the lad's face, but there was no sound or response. So he returned to meet him and told him, "The lad has not awakened."

When Elisha came into the house, behold the lad was dead and laid on his bed. So he entered and shut the door behind them both and prayed to the LORD. And he went up and lay on the child, and put his mouth on his mouth and his eyes on his eyes and his hands on his hands, and he stretched himself on him; and the flesh of the child became warm. Then he returned and walked in the house once back and forth, and went up and stretched himself on him; and the lad sneezed seven times and the lad opened his eyes. He called Gehazi and said, "Call this Shunammite." So he called her. And when she came in to him, he said, "Take up your son." Then she went in and fell at his feet and bowed herself to the ground, and she took up her son and went out (2 Kings 4:31-37).

The child comes back to life.

The story is not a typical, cut-and-dried healing. It has little triumphalism. Elisha's underling tries to revive the boy with his magic staff and fails. The expected solution does not work. The holy man prays to God and then lays himself on the boy, eye to eye, mouth to mouth. Not yet enough. He has to work with it—go downstairs, walk around, come back, and do it again. He matches himself, body to body to that child. Praying, walking, breathing, going back. Doing it again. We sense that this is an uncertain process, that Elisha is groping, trying one thing, then another.

How do we fully become ourselves? By knowing the false gods of the world and resisting them, certainly. But the workings of God are less in the resistance itself than in finding the shape of our own particular incarnation of resistance. We must find a way to live out the resistance that feels like our own face, our own flesh.

Here is what I know about dreams: Dreams can make us live, but they can also leave a hole inside us when they die. Some of them come true. But it's the ones that don't come true, the ones that go down in flames, that can kill us. But here is the secret: If we embrace them and take them into our holy room, if we sit and learn what they have to teach us, they may just help us live.

The wonderful, audacious hope of new life pervades scripture. The enslaved are brought from oppression into the land of abundance where they rebuild their lives. Jacob struggles with an angel—and emerges with a wound, a new name, and a different future. Jesus returns from the dead and unleashes a new way of life.

Yet loss is everywhere—we read about death and failure in every book of the Bible. To live, we must learn to touch that failure with our own face—our eyes, our mouth. Once we move beyond our pat theologies, political paradigms, or explanations and justifications for our failures, we stand on new ground. That new ground will shape us if we work with it. Then, inexplicably, the joy erupts because despite the failures and the deaths, we know that we are in touch with the holy path. Even if our lives have a clunky, experimental quality that strains us, they also possess a clarity that shows us the way. Although the story doesn't tell us, we know that the child and the Shunammite woman were never again the same. One who has witnessed the power of resurrection will never again view death in the same fearful way.

The stories and dreams I share in this book are not insightful stories of triumph or victory. They are about places that lie between strong vision and necessary or reluctant compromise. They are about failure. When we try to live into cultural alternatives, we hit hard stuff. No matter how fervent, our personal struggles with our own internal demons—or external demons like patriarchy, classism, racism, or materialism—will not always succeed. These behaviors run deep in us and will rise up again and again. Discovering this can be unimaginably painful. And so grieving our losses becomes part of our spiritual work. When we try to break down barriers in the world and in our lives, we are living in uncharted territory and will encounter failure.

I never expected to be here—unsettled, sometimes looking over my shoulder at so many precious and lost moments. I expected to always look forward, always be moving somewhere. I yearn for some fruition of my dreams: a time when racism and the earth are healed, when every child is loved to his or her full potential in every way, when my lover and best friend never doubts his beauty, when I am the person on this earth whom I long to be. I long for the certainty that my children possess—that they will save the frogs.

I did not choose these dreams of mine. They were given to me. I'm sure of it. The Spirit beckoned them, whispering: "Dee Dee, this is part of my vocation for you. Strive to make these dreams a reality. I will go with you." And with that God-inspired passion at my back, I plunged ahead, doing my best to be faithful to what was asked. Truth be told, I expected to bring at least one dream to fruition—given all the heart that I was willing to pour in and all the need and the rightness of the causes.

It hasn't worked like that. There have been no triumphs. People and causes important to me have died when they didn't need to while my heart railed, *God, it was not their time!* Beautiful places and dwellings on earth that meant everything to me have been torn down or destroyed. I can look back in my own life and see times that will never come again. Instead of giving my children a healthier world, I am apprehensive for the ecological changes that will occur in their lifetimes.

I sit with my friends, some of whom are four decades farther along this riddled path of life. They humor me. To them, I am so young. "Ah, I would love to be fifty again," they smile at me from their older lives. Now they struggle with physical and mental diminishment and significant loss of independence. One cocks his head at me and says, "Ah, at fifty, I started an entire new life!" I am too young to feel so daunted.

It's not as if I have ever had illusions about changing the world, but I have thought that I might shift one corner of it. I did not expect to be spiritually disheartened so soon. Here I am, emptied and less resilient than a few years ago, as if I stand on the verge of throwing in some cosmic towel. My peers resonate. Some shift we can't name makes it hard to keep our spiritual grounding. There must be something more to this time in our lives than crossing our fingers as we watch the next few generations grow up lovely yet fragile behind us.

Inwardly, I argue with God. *I wasn't the one who brought to birth all those dreams! Do you bring me to these disheartened and hollow places to teach me?* What possible will of God is there in these lovely or powerful things dying in my hands? Yet just as the skeletal trunks of trees emerge after a soft snow begins to melt, the truth is there. We have the opportunity to redefine our lives in significant ways. It is not all about going forward. It is not about youth or health. It is not even about us. We confront once more the question of what we are living for. Perhaps for the first time, our lives offer us enough experiences of loss and failure that we can actually learn the art of living.

I recognize—much more intensely than before—all that people are asked to live through. Aging, like parenting or birth, is something we cannot understand until we are in it. In these middle years, I appreciate the ambiguity and complexity in every choice. No matter where we stand, life assails us. I've experienced few big spiritual breakthroughs. Glimpses of grace, yes. Love everywhere, yes. Beauty piercing through the broken places—that too. I circle back around and sit at the feet of the story again, that old prophet and that feisty woman. I have an unshakable hunch that it has more to teach me, that it holds a lesson for this time in my life. Those things God promises to bring to fruition die inexplicably and impossibly. Why would God give us these visions if they aren't meant to flourish? How do we grieve? How do we find the spirit of the Shunammite woman to argue about it all?

I am convinced that the root of our denial about our own participation in racism and our disempowerment to address the economic and ecological exploitation of the world or whatever our points of struggle is that we have lost touch with whole parts of ourselves, the sad and wounded parts, the parts that have also been hurt by the injustice. We have not been able to cry or lament. Grief opens the door and carries us over the threshold to a place of different wisdom. Then the real work of God begins—the carving and sanding that shape us. We have to find our own answers.

When those answers come, they will not fit our perfect ideologies. They will be born of concession and compromise, of trying first one new model and then another. They will instill in us a deep, almost mystical, appreciation of grace. When those answers come, they will reshape our hearts. We will be cloaked in gratitude—specific gratitudes that spring from our particular, life-giving moments. Ultimately this gratitude opens the only path that can call us home to our true and authentic selves.

Chapter 20

One Light Burning

Acertain fragility marks our lives in this particular moment in time. Traditional forms of community and rooted ways of living are dying and need intentional nurturing. Human domination of the planet causes changing weather and temperature patterns. The political climate is at its most polarized, and the global economic system thrives on wealth disparities. Resilience has never been more necessary. We are all trying to find a place to stand.

My own path is peppered with moments that make me less than proud. I reflect on them, wondering if I could be more large-hearted and wiser if given another chance. I would respond differently to my children at certain moments. I would have made different decisions with coworkers. I would have tried to be less serious or critical. I am grateful for each new day that offers the opportunity for repentance, change, and living in a different way. Life unravels and reweaves unexpected patterns of love and loss around us.

I recorded in my journal a Mardi Gras celebration from a few years back:

It is mid-February and a busy week for us celebrating types—Mardi Gras on Tuesday, Ash Wednesday and the Chinese New Year, Valentine's Day looming.

Last night, Will came home to our Mardi Gras dinner feeling fragile and close to the edge. The menu was decadent and messy—goopy, greasy barbequed chicken and beignets for dessert.

We made masks. Thea painted a mask for her constant companion and stuffed animal, Really Doggie. Luke made my mask and his own (both stunning). After supper, though it was very late, we got out the face paints, donned our masks, and put on music. We danced to three songs, wild with partying. Will, barely holding it together, left, and the three of us continued to dance.

Then my children and I settled down, lit candles, and thought about how Jesus might like us to change during Lent. Though young, they readily grasped the idea. I told them that I wanted to be a better, more patient mother and raise my voice less. Secretly I added, *I want to pray more, to use this time to grow my interior life.*

At first, Thea came up with ideas for Luke: "Luke shouldn't call me bad words like *stupid.*" I affirmed that and then pressed her—what would she like to change about herself? "I want to work better with Luke."

Luke followed suit. "I will play better with Thea, and when Daddy feels bad, I will stay away from him." (I took this to mean not antagonize him and be wild.)

Later, Will came home, still fragile, upset, edgy. Luke asked him if he is "hyper." Then he told me, "See, I did what I promised—I stayed away and didn't bother him."

We are not compensating. We are carrying life. And life includes things like anxiety and depression and loss and grief. We are carrying it. We are not denying it. We are releasing it and giving it no power. We are dancing; we are singing.

So much of what we wrest from life in this middle season comes from not giving events, words, or thoughts power over us. We refuse to let failures, losses, and fears define us; we refuse to be silent on significant topics like depression, money, and love. We refuse to always answer "fine" when we are asked how we are.

How can we have authentic lives and authentic relationships if we continue to gloss over our struggles with small, well-intended white lies designed to make everything okay? The reality is that we live our lives and raise our families in a world of deep chasms between rich and poor, a world riddled with exploitations that we have created. Such a world is dangerous to navigate and full of pain.

We choose what power to give things. Once when I went to pick my son up from his preschool, his teacher took me aside to tell me a child had brought in a knife. The child had showed it to some male classmates, including my son. Two of the students told the teacher, and the situation was handled—the parent called, the kid taken home. In my journal to Luke, I pondered power.

> You haven't mentioned the knife to me, though I've casually asked what things you remember from your day. It seems that the incident did not register. You have not added it to your inventory of the day, for which I am grateful.
>
> I am taking my cues about today from you. Already, I am trying to forget it. I am not trying to make it a sign of what my rural, white, racist self fears a Head Start program with low-income kids in the middle of the city could be. I am trying not to cave to my racist or classist conditioning. I am refusing to give it power. A classmate showed you a knife, open and lethal in his palm.
>
> I'll say instead that the grownups handled it well and quickly. That you carried home no fear. That all flesh went home whole and unscathed.
>
> Say that we saw the knife. Say that we put it away.
>
> Say that you came home running, joyful, waiting for lightning bugs, summer rolling before you. Give it no power.

This is not to say that a moment such as that—a child bringing a knife to preschool—does not touch us with the reminder of fragility and possible loss. But it can also remind us of resilience and open a door into gratitude.

Several years ago, during the final weeks of Lent, as the wind howled over the snow-strewn city streets outside, close friends gathered in my living room to pray for healing of Will's persistent depression. It was a biblical and revolutionary step. It was also terrifying.

Will and I had prayed—constantly. We had also tried most of what the medical world had to offer—extensive counseling, therapies, retreats, medications, and more medications. Still the dark, anxious thoughts dogged his spirit. We hoped to cast the demons out. In an unexpected way, we did. Years later, I read my account of that day.

We had a fresh coating of snow, so everything outside our windows was black and white and blue sky and, at this point in the month, a small, brilliant half-moon.

By the time I got downstairs, the kids had laid out an elaborate party with all of their stuffed animals. Luke had located and distributed party hats, blowers (carefully placed in front of every animal in the circle), and balloons (blown up with the bicycle pump). It was an Easter party, and there was an elaborate egg hunt that involved hiding conversation Valentine hearts all over the house.

I have felt this entire Lent that we were moving toward something, that something was going to give. Moving toward something hard and something healing. Something will die, and something will live. I have struggled so that Will will live.

Luke had his own children's Bible, ready to instruct his animals in the real meaning of Easter, wanting to read them the Resurrection story. (If only he could read.) We are gathering tonight for resurrection, I thought.

Then it was evening. Will was home to set the house in order in his quick and focused way that I can never really mimic, and it was time to take the kids to a friend's house and put out luminaries on our long, dark path. Luke and I carried seven luminaries into the wind to guide our friends inside.

Friends gathered to pray out the shadows in Will's courageous and tired heart. Together we laid an altar. Though no one had been asked, everyone brought a talisman. The oil lamp was made by hermit Richard, who years ago confided to Will that he felt Will was called to battle the demons in his family generations before. Shane brought a cloth woven in a community in India that is sacred to him—a community of healing. This became our altar cloth. Donna brought the oil of anointing. Bernadette brought water from Lourdes that she had mixed with the water of our own home. Johanna brought a clay pot and soil from Chimayo, a sacred site in New Mexico.

My friends and I began praying, and the prayer became a prayer for Will as part of generations that have been bound by this demon in their family, whatever one calls it. And the prayer became an invocation of who we know Will to be—brilliant teacher, compassionate leader, brother, friend, spiritual mentor, music-maker, prophet offering renewed vision. And the prayer became recognition of the powers that wish each one of us to stay bound. And the prayer became a prayer that my children be shielded from the demon that has dogged the generations before them and that I embrace my own funny wirings. The prayer became larger than any of us.

The winds of the Spirit howled around our house over the white, silent snow. Until at last the long sigh at the end of prayer came, the space when all has been said, and it was time to carry the children back, sleepy in arms, down the long path.

"Look," Luke said, almost asleep. "Can you believe that candle is still burning?"

Sometimes our hope is as small as one light burning in the great night. After that night, Will's depression lifted. It has never gone away completely. But Will and I have learned to see the wisdom that living with depression has given us. We have learned to appreciate the courage of keeping one light burning.

Which is the greater healing—that depression will never again shadow Will's brave and Spirit-filled heart or that he is able cling resolutely to God and the transforming power of the gospel even as he lives in the ups and downs of depression?

Which is the greater healing—that I begin to understand my brokenness and somehow live with it as a part of me or that I never experience brokenness in my life? The second would make me strong, but the first would make me wiser and more compassionate. The spiritual growth that comes with confronting and releasing loss is ultimately a more powerful testimony than a life in which there is no such loss.

The earth turns, and we turn with it. We hold that which we did not choose in our arms. We learn to say its name.

Chapter 21

Coming Home to Ourselves

Twentieth-century author J. R. R. Tolkien, creator of *The Lord of the Rings* trilogy, *The Hobbit*, and other works, had a dream. He bemoaned England's lack of ancient cultural mythology and wanted to create stories large enough to fill that void. The complex history he built in his writings embraced fictional historical lineages of multiple genres of characters (elves, dwarves, humans of different ilks, hobbits, and wizards). Tolkien even built several distinct languages for his characters based on extant Welsh, Finnish, and other languages. His work was in every way a powerful and daunting intellectual vision. Part of the inspiration but also the burden of Tolkien's writing were significant losses he witnessed. The slow, inexorable destruction of English countryside by industrialization before and after World War I makes its way into his writing. The brutality of battle, even righteous battle, is inescapable.

Tolkien was one of a group of four men who dubbed themselves the T.C.B.S. (standing for "Tea Club and Barrovian Society," due to their predilection for meeting in tea rooms). They vowed to remain friends, and with the academic fervor and hubris of young scholars, they also shared the common intellectual vision of creating a modern mythology.

Before they could do so, World War I took all of them to the battlefields of Europe; two never returned. Geoffrey Bache Smith was one of them. He gave Tolkien a task in a letter sent before his death in France in November 1916: "My chief consolation is that if I am scuppered tonight there will still be left a member of the great T.C.B.S. to voice what I dreamed and what we all agreed upon. . . . May God bless you my dear John Ronald, and may you say the things I have tried to say long after I am not there to say them." Tolkien's writing was sparked, at least in part, by the significant loss of his friend.

Telling the tales became the work of Tolkien's life, but his are not stories of inexorable triumph. *The Lord of the Rings* is infused with a deep sense of passage and loss and entire civilizations moving on. The time of the elves is waning, and Tolkien makes it clear that theirs was a time of unsurpassed wisdom, beauty, and healing. Though the quest to destroy the ring of evil is successful, those who attempt it leave this age prematurely.

My grandmother, widowed for decades, used to stare out her bedroom window, looking over the landscape of the family farm. It had completely changed face during the decades of her tenure from small fields and sharecropper shacks to large, machinated fields as far as the eye could see. Widowed in her sixties, she lived to be almost one hundred with mind sharp and wit intact. She had the unenviable experience of outliving every one of her good friends.

"Can you imagine what it is like to have none of your friends left—no one who knew you as a young person?" she'd asked me pointedly. I pondered that loss. My friends hold the events of my life in a way that none of my family or children can. I cannot imagine navigating the world without those who know me well.

My generation is spinning in a vortex of change, and at the center is the sucking echo of things passing—community affiliations, habits of human gathering and interactions, aspects of nature. Can they be replaced? Will I find them again? I am learning that everything passes and must be let go. Poet Denise Levertov captures my feelings in her poignant poem-meditation "Once Only."

All which, because it was
flame and song and granted us

joy, we thought we'd do, be, revisit,
turns out to have been what it was
that *once*, only; every invitation
did not begin
a series, a build-up: the marvelous
    did happen in our lives, our stories
    are not drab with its absence: but don't
expect now to return for more. Whatever more
there will be will be
unique as those were unique. Try
to acknowledge the next
song in its body-halo of flames as utterly
present, as now or never.

The question becomes how do we engage the loss? How do we harvest it? In this respect, the story of Elisha and this woman of Shunem provides a beautiful example. She holds her firstborn till he dies and then leaves him in the holy room, stretched right in the middle of the holy man's bed. She doesn't mind putting death in the middle of the holy space.

Dead dreams, passions, and longings lie in our holy rooms. No trite religious truisms apply. They were not "meant" to die. There is no greater good or purpose of God served by their deaths. These deaths are not some unseen part of a great plan of which we are ignorant, building toward some final glory. They are not God's inscrutable will at work. The questions God asks of us when we lay these things before God is riveting and simple: "What will you make of this? What are ways you can craft life from this death?"

I falter in answering, and God gets a bit more pointed. "Are you choosing life? Or are you choosing to be stuck? Are you going to make something of this pain? Can you make it teach you?"

"I don't know, " I whisper. I'd rather just fade away somewhere and live a quiet, comfortable life in this consumer world where I don't think about these kinds of things any more. All my choices feel circumscribed now. I am not where I thought I would be. The world keeps spinning; the problems seem intractable. My own hours, efforts, and capabilities seem small and unworthy of any dream toward which I'd point them.

A few years ago, Will and I were in a fairly serious car accident. Car totaled, broken bones, a brush with mortality. For both of us, the accident unexpectedly shook all kinds of things loose—large, unexpected questions about life, unsettling memories about family, demons of guilt and insecurity. Decades of Christian conditioning primed me to puzzle over God's hand in this situation, even though I distrust any theology that fits every circumstance into God's omnipotent plan or intent. Lots of theology started coming at me from friends and family who wished to comfort me. Yes, of course I was grateful that our two children were not with us at the time. I heard all of the (true) counsel that we only lost a car, mere property—but at the time, to lose our first nice car ever, the one that was to last us a full ten more years, seemed like a palpable blow. I was groping around for some "will" of God.

Will heard me out with concern in his grave eyes and then made a quiet comment that changed my thinking. "I'll never believe that God caused that accident. I don't believe it was part of some great plan. However, I believe that God asks me, having lived through the accident, to wrest some learning from it that will help it be spiritually redemptive and empowering. I am the one to make meaning from it and to give it its meaning. As I do that, God grows more present to me."

Sometimes these middle years feel like one big car wreck, and I just want to get off the highway and sit in a ditch. But then I think of Will's words, and I ask myself a question: *Can I do the work to learn something that makes me stronger and more merciful?*

Youth and the experiences of our first few decades can carry a special sheen. It will pass, and when it does, we will have to work to avoid apathy, jadedness, or a complete relinquishment of things that we once felt were important. Loss is real. Death is inescapable. Both will happen, and both will have deep spiritual repercussions. Our culture laughingly terms this time in life as the midlife crisis, a phrase rife with connotations of some self-generated drama, but it is nothing to mock. A midlife crisis brings disorientation and uncertainty as we find ourselves groping for a plumb line.

If the current social indicators hold true—people will stay in a job an average of nine years and in a career field an average of fifteen—then we are becoming a transitional people. The family farm, the small town, the rural community, the backwater niche—these ways of life are disappearing. We are probably not going to live in the extended family household like my grandmother assumed, at least not without great intention. And as life unfolds in this era, a question is going to circle around again, always breathing at our backs, sometimes grabbing us by the shoulders and staring us down: What are we living for?

The gift of this season is that we finally have enough experiences of loss and failure to learn from the terrain. Midlife offers a rich understanding of everything that people live through. Life is hard— and we must find the place in it that looks and feels like us.

In his book *Secrets in the Dark: A Life in Sermons*, Frederick Buechner reminds us of the alchemy from pain to spiritual growth:

> To bury your pain is a way of surviving your pain and therefore by no means to be dismissed out of hand. It is a way that I venture to say has at one time or another served and continues to serve all of us well. But it is not a way of growing. It is not a way of moving through adolescence into adulthood. If you manage to put behind you the painful things that happen to you as if they never really happened or didn't really matter all that much when they did, then the deepest and most human things you have in you to become are not apt to happen either.[1]

The loss and the failures of life happen so that we can come home more truly to ourselves.

But how, I ask myself, *do I possibly find the way?*

Chapter 22

The Door of Authenticity

The most powerful truth in scripture is the story of death and new life—told hundreds of ways. Some stories we know well. Others are almost buried or overshadowed by Jesus' resurrection story in the Gospels.

New life is the truth Cain, brother and murderer, lives out when he is spared death and settles east of Eden, wearing a mark of protection from God. New life comes in a flood, a dove, and an earth reborn in covenant. We see it in a tower unmade, scattering people so that different languages and cultures rise in all their richness. We see it in Sarai and Abram, going forth from Ur to an unknown place, cloaked in new names and identities. We see new life in Hagar and her infant son, cast out by her mistress into the harsh and deadly grip of the desert but saved by the eye of God, "a God who sees" (Gen. 16:13). New life speaks when Huldah, the old prophet woman, last of the learned ones, reads the dusty scrolls and brings the heart of the people back to God. We see it in Bathsheba, pawn of kings and generals and victim of their lusts, breaking open a powerful man's heart with confession and birthing a child of wisdom, Solomon. We see new life in Paul, shattered to blindness on the road and then seeing again. We see it in the unnamed woman in the book of Revelation, birthing a child in the face of a dragon.

The stories rain down. In the Christian tradition, these holy writings are arranged in an arc toward creating things new—new heaven and new earth. That arc begins with Eden, (which offers the narrative of the beauty, oneness, and love of God that we know in our bones but cannot live into) and ends with the revelation of an enfleshed God who empowers bands of followers with a Spirit that will not be held back and scatters them throughout the world, spreading like breath and fire. The Bible speaks of a God who gathers the people back in, the last first and the first last, wiping every tear from our eyes. Death and resurrection are scrawled messily and unexpectedly into our lives. People survive horrendous things, and they make that pain the cornerstone gift of their new life. We know these people. They are around us. They have looked into my eyes and told me their stories.

A woman's seven-year-old daughter is murdered by a stranger. Later she seeks out the disturbed young man in prison and comes to care for him. Next to me in the pew is a committed believer and thoughtful man, father of foster children. Only after years do I hear the story of how he once drank, and one night, possessed by that demon drink, he shot the child of his neighbor—a church community member and his friend. That terrible pain had to be reconciled between them. How are there such miracles of heart in our midst?

Our loved one gets cancer and dies too young. Our friend slams a relational door in our face and is lost to us suddenly and inexplicably. Our bodies change in shape and sometimes betray us. Our offspring, those entities into which we have poured the deepest parts of ourselves—ministries, communities, children, covenanted relationships of love, cherished vocations—turn on us or disappear.

We have all felt left behind as life moved on. And somehow, we have made something new of the pain, groping in the shards of loss for the materials, creating almost in spite of ourselves. What is this Spirit that continues on despite all our experience and best judgment?

In his last recorded song, Rastafarian musician Bob Marley claimed that all he ever sang were songs of freedom—"redemption songs." Sometimes I look closely at the lives around me and catch my breath at all the redemption songs whose lyrics are etched in real lives. I want to hear those songs, raw and transparent, heartbreaking in their loveliness. I don't want that song to be varnished with spiritual triumphalism or subsumed under some all-knowing, never-thwarted will of God. I have no patience for platitudes about God's great intent spoken over tragedies in our lives. I don't want our pain to be used for trite lessons about God or God's will. Life is hard enough without placating its challenge, its mystery, and its pain. I long for the simple declaration of faith that matches my messy and uneven life: "I do believe; help my unbelief" (Mark 9:24). I love that this bald utterance of confused helplessness, this certainty of belief and the yearning for belief, was uttered by a parent seeking healing for his child from Jesus.

What is the relationship between redemption and resurrection? I puzzle over the two, turning them over in my head. Are they siblings? They seem somehow connected. To me, redemption is the lovelier one. It speaks of bringing things back that appeared lost, of never giving up on the possibility of anything or anyone joining that arc toward goodness. It gives old things, marginal things, and frayed things new life and goes beyond that to make them part of the central pattern. It is spiritual up-cycling—a kind of recycling that imbues old and tired pieces of our lives with new meanings. It is bringing people back from the edge and giving them a role in the community, pulling in elements at the margins and making them whole and vital again.

But resurrection is more dramatic, more impossible. The finality of death allows no returns. We all know redemption stories, but few of us have witnessed resurrections. Resurrections are rarer.

When I was in my twenties, thirties, and forties, my life still revolved around accomplishment, even if in a kinder, gentler way. I went to college at a high-achiever institution, and I wanted to be another high achiever, whatever my field might be. I didn't need to be famous—but I wanted to be seen as capable, wise, and influential in my own little niche. And maybe if all had gone smoothly, life would have stayed there, with me believing subconsciously in merit.

But that bit didn't quite work out, so I live with less illusion. I'm an average writer and not particularly insightful parent or mentor.

I've gained a bit too much weight, and my daughter likes to fiddle with the wrinkles at my elbow. I can be a black-and-white thinker, a pretentious and judgmental faux-intellectual, and a control freak. I have spent a lot of life dreaming about justice, but I have not paid the costs of integrity I might have. But I believe that the pain I confront is the way I find the path leading to who I really, truly am. It leads me to the door of authenticity.

It is important to note that in the Shunem tale, the moment of power never comes in full-fledged glory. As miracles go, this is a clunky story. First, Elisha sends Gehazi, his right-hand man, with Elisha's own staff. Gehazi returns to his master and says that he has failed. The prophet goes in and shuts the door on the two of them, lies on the child, and prays, but, as we know, there is no resurrection. Nothing is redeemed.

And then the story turns physical in its yearning for new life. The Holy Man paces the room, climbs again upon the bed where the child who is a gift of God lies dead. Elisha stretches himself on top of the boy, actually matching his face to that of the child—putting his mouth on the child's mouth, his eyes on the child's eyes, his hands on the child's hands. I catch my breath at the mixture of love and recoil I feel at Elisha's courage to touch the dead. After putting his body on top of the boy's body, Elisha feels the boy's flesh grow warm, some imperceptible shift of energy. Was it real? He walks around the house. Perhaps he finds himself struggling with failure, doubt, and sadness. Elisha returns to the room, climbs on the bed, and does it all again—eyelid brushing eyelid, mouth on mouth, hand against cold hand.

This is an incredibly physical story in its telling, its details. I don't think that is by accident. This story tries to offer some truth across the culture and the centuries. It wants us to feel the touch of this story in our flesh. It wants us to see the prophet struggling. It wants us to taste the possibility of failure, death, and no miracle.

I page through my journal, and the same old refrains catch me. I am always vowing to structure my writing, to detach from a compulsion to meet the expectations of others, to be infinitely patient with my children, to spend more time in my holy room, to live a more prayer-centered and just life. I am often raging, pleading for my next niche, or lamenting what now lives in the past. The reflections turn and turn on themselves. I write, "Sometimes my life feels like the same melody, old and inescapable." I am lying on the body again. I am returning to it. This is part of the risk. It is part of the belief in the possibility of healing.

We know there are untold stories of other children in Shunem—children who were not brought back to life. Those stories never made it into the chronicles of the kings. We know too well these stories of the children who are not saved. But after two repetitions of the body prayer of the prophet, this child is saved. This is the child who comes back to life.

Love has something to do with the miracle. Our capacity to love each other may be the only thing that brings miracles. Elisha loves the child he was responsible for calling into life. His yearning, his reach for healing and resurrection are fueled by love for this child. We can enact that same miracle. George Vaillant, a psychiatrist at Harvard, insists that our ability to mature and ultimately to age well hinges directly on our capacity to love. "When we are old, our lives become the sum of all whom we have loved. It is important not to waste anyone. One task of living out the last half of life is excavating and recovering all of those whom we loved in the first half. Thus, the recovery of lost loves becomes an important way in which the past affects the present."[1] We need to make our peace with those we have loved and those who have loved us.

How do we live in a way that keeps our hearts open to new possibilities of redemption and resurrection? Many stories show us that redemption comes from strange and unexpected messengers. Redemption can even be accomplished through flaws, shortcomings, weaknesses, and evil. The possible avenues of redemption are limitless. Though we may find it hard to believe, our failures and shortcomings are actually the most significant and necessary parts of our redemption. How might we view our obstacles as the primary shapers of our authentic selves? They mold us, providing the only path we can take toward understanding our full selves.

How do we follow the Shunammite woman and Elisha? How do we embrace our dead and beloved dreams and people in redemptive ways that lead toward that mystery of resurrection? Like her, we have to be willing to argue through it all, to resist, to fighting when we have to. It is spiritual death to deny our struggles—or to layer pieties over them. This is where our theologies have not served us. To recognize and give voice to our experience is a way of taking our loss to the heart of our life and setting it in the holy place. Like Elisha, we must commit to being present and showing up no matter what.

Once, after a crisis in my life, prayer felt like the most vapid exercise in the world. I sat in front of my burning candle; I read powerful scriptures. I waited for the Spirit, but I felt nothing. "All I'm doing," I told my spiritual director, "is showing up." Nothing was going on that I could see, and I wanted to throw in every towel and admit that faith was just a figment of my imagination.

Showing up has its place, but that act alone carries no promise of renewal. We do not know if or when renewal might come. But sometimes we summon the creative and working forces that redeem and return us to life purely by persistence—showing up and staying in the room. Most of the losses in our lives have no explanations—or none that will satisfy us or heal the depth of our wounds. There is no God-will behind why my beloved struggles with depression or why a powerful ministry that many people built over four decades faltered and went up in flames or why cancer has recurred in the young, healthy, praying body of my friend four times. These are not sufferings ordained by heaven, but they are ours to carry.

Through our persistence—our showing up—something amazing can start to happen. We may not be able to make peace with our loss, but we can find the capacity to take it in and sit with it. We put the dead thing in the holy room, shut the door, and pray with it, just the two of us. We lie on top of it and cover it with our entire selves. We open ourselves to the love around us, to any crumb of love present.

Then ever so slowly a shaft of light filters through a window, a crack in the roof, and we find ourselves beginning to release the loss. Not because we have answers. Not because we are satisfied. And not because we have given in or given up. Perhaps we release it because we have honored the beauty of the loss well. We have matched it up to our own body, eye, mouth, hand. We have tasted all that it is, and our love of it brings some warmth back. We release it because something tells us that it is time and that we are strong enough. And when it is time, the release is not a betrayal, and it doesn't feel like one. We feel free—we no longer carry the dead body of our loss—and we understand that God shaped us and taught us in that holy room.

I once confessed to my friend Scotty, a woman who had recently buried her life partner, lost her church, and struggled to recover from a stroke, that I wasn't feeling spiritually strong. At the time, I felt dull and fragile and lost. Scotty responded in a way I will never forget.

Look for the shafts of light. I am eighty, and I was able to go by myself to my home place and to go swimming in the creek I love. And then I rode back with my grandchildren who were singing melodious harmony, and I listened to their amazing music, thinking, *I am eightysomething, and I never thought I would live this long, and here I am, riding down the road with wonderful music.* Dee Dee, it's not the stuff of your life that matters; it's the shafts of light! And when we get together, I hope that you will tell me about those shafts of light and not anything else.

Chapter 23

Finding Shafts of Light

For the first half of my life, I never practiced gratitude.

Sure, I gave thanks in my prayers. I was conscious that I should be thankful for the beauty of the earth and when things went well in my life. But I did not know the secret of gratitude, and I did not practice being grateful as a discipline. Somewhere in the midst of life, I'd shouldered duty and responsibility. I wanted to be worthy, to do a good job, and to be one who could be trusted. I wanted to be productive. But I never donned the cloak of gratitude.

So I did not know that gratitude changes everything. Gratitude allows us to become—or even makes us become—our best selves. Gratitude carves our souls, and it is perhaps the most powerful spiritual tool we wield. The practice of gratitude is a discipline, and by that I mean a cultivated habit. A habit cultivated in spite of our natural leanings and instincts. It's a habit we may need to work at, to hone, and to bring to our consciousness.

Saying "thank you" comes naturally to me. Even a year ago, I would have shunned the idea or even the suggestion that I was not a grateful person. But the daily practice of looking for and celebrating experiences—actually marking them in memory, pausing to lift them up, and looking through them like a glass in the light—does not. A spirit of gratitude differs from being frequently thankful for specific events or items in our lives. A spirit of gratitude creates a prayer for a change of vision. Instead of being caught in the heavy currents of life and tumbling down the flood-swollen river, we float to the surface. There, we glimpse a shock of lily on the bank, a graceful tree branch. Yes, we are going down a river, and most things are out of our control. But to go down that river consciously, looking for beauty and wonder, means that we actually *see* it.

My spirit these middle years has been caught in responsibility, in all the change of children growing and elders aging, people moving away or dying, and the world of work morphing. It is easy for fear to come in. I wonder, *What if we cannot do what we have committed to? What if our body and capacity change? What if we are no longer loved?*

Gratitude is the great demon-vanquisher. We cannot be grateful and carry emotions of fear, anxiety, or anger. Our wiring is not capable of it. Moreover, gratitude changes our place in the chain of being. Gratitude by its very nature makes us a recipient. We are not the giver. That weight is off our shoulders. Gifts are bestowed upon us, and we recognize them. We do not have to produce or be worthy. Instead, moments come into our unsuspecting and outstretched hands. Our job is simply to unwrap them.

Two years ago, I began the discipline of writing down daily moments of beauty. I gave myself a quota of five each day. I found the practice challenging, so I kept a white notebook with me at all times. I wrote about the angle of the robin's head, the five-year-old dressed up for ballet, the three men who always stand outside the liquor store as neighborhood ambassadors. I wrote about the golden beauty of an egg yolk and the way my mother's cornflower-blue eyes look out a window. I jotted down red-skinned potatoes.

I began to thank my beloveds. I offered thank-yous for doing chores, for helping me solve a technical obstacle, for their habit of cracking jokes, for the music they played that filled the house. I became more attuned to catching every silent effort toward goodness, beauty, and helpfulness that they made. Like every good habit in my life, the notebook writing became erratic. But by then, the power of gratitude had seeded itself in me. I understood what gratitude could offer my life.

My gratitude writing was such a far cry from a few years ago when I'd biked to a friend's house, suffocated by blues and anxiety. I wanted to write the mood away, but I simply wrote myself into deeper worry and desperation. I was in a dark place. My friend came outside where I was writing and joined me in my place of solitude that was actually loneliness. "Let's just write ten things you are grateful for," she said, her eyes full of love and grief for me. Each one was a struggle. She sat there coaxing me, blue pen in hand, so I had to produce a list. Even as I named them, I did not feel their joy. Every word was forced, and every item had a thousand "buts" around it. When I left, the list felt more like an indictment of my small-heartedness than a mantra.

So it is with wonder that I now find myself in this new place, where gratitude steps in unasked. To get here, I had to retrain my eyes. They were accustomed to searching for concerns, hard-edged stones to turn over and chafe in my palm. Gratitude displaced my anxiety. Will said to me recently, "I wonder if you are addicted to anxiety." Midlife shifts *have* made me anxious in a way that I never was before, but when I am looking for and practicing gratitude, anxiety loses its hold. In a world that stands ready to hand me beauty, can I hold on to anxiety?

Anxiety assumes a world filled with harm and speaks to all we cannot control. While we have little control and much can harm us, gratitude also offers a large piece of truth: The world is here to offer us gifts, and our love and support of one another brings those gifts to life. If we willingly engage in the looking, the world shows us beauty every day.

And it does demand looking.

I'd been training myself in anxiety; but when I began to train my eyes to see blessing, my world changed. Searching for blessing erased an old, tired line I'd started to whine to myself about my failures and missteps. That whine verged on a victim script. Gratitude has no use for victim scripts.

Gratitude also knocks down victimization's ugly first cousin— entitlement. People feel their relationships owe them, society owes them, the "rich" or the "poor" owe them. Children, including my own, feel they are entitled to so many material things: electronics and cell phones, trendy clothes and choice over how to spend their time. First-Worlders feel entitled to consumptive lifestyles that resist all ecological limits.

Gratitude crumbles these fortresses by reminding us of redemption and miracle. I have learned a refrain from people born into less powerful social statuses than my own (a fact I do not think is coincidental to this wisdom). I've heard it spill from the mouths of migrant workers and prisoners, jobless immigrants and poor, dark-skinned mothers. They give thanks. *Thank you Lord for waking me up this morning, blood flowing warm in my veins.* They are thankful for shelter and for food. They are thankful for all the things I, as a person of means and some power, expect every day.

Practicing gratitude lowered the volume of my brain, opened my eyes, and made me confront my own life. It shoved aside my fears and anxieties about the future and made room for the beauty of the present. Gradually, I learned that our difficult passages help us become our most authentic selves, but the alchemist that shapes us into those selves is gratitude.

Our gratitude help us discover our sacred, holy life. We do not have to be grateful for our losses. That is unnaturally hard and too much to ask. But even in great loss, we can still find beauty. Continuing to practice gratitude will help us realize how loss has created within us a new spirit. We are not entitled to anything. All is gift. Once we know this, we can let so many stones fall from our hands.

Anne Voskamp, a writer and mother homeschooling six on a farm in Canada, unpacks the complex elements of gratitude in her wonderful book, *One Thousand Gifts: A Dare to Live Fully Right Where You Are,* an incredible plunge into gratitude. A friend challenged her to write one thousand things she was grateful for. The practice changed her life, and she notes that gratitude gives us more time by putting us completely in the present. Entering into a space of paying attention slows time by increasing our awareness.[1]

Ultimately, gratitude and the daily, constant attentiveness it demanded brought me home to myself. In many ways, it brought me back to life or, rather, it brought life back to me.

That boy came back to life. Things in our lives circle around. They are redeemed. We love some part of them, and they breathe again.

Chapter 24

Some New Face

The boy comes back to life.

Scripture contains a generous smattering of actual, died-and-came-back-to-life resurrection stories beyond the big Gospel block-buster. Lazarus, Jairus's daughter, and the widow of Nain's son are perhaps the most well-known because they were raised by Jesus, and their stories appear in the Gospels. But First and Second Kings contain no fewer than three resurrection stories, including the Shunammite's son. The prophet Elisha even raises another corpse *after* he himself is dead with the mere touch of his postmortem bones! (See 2 Kings 13:20-21.)

We are never told of the lives that continue after resurrection. The accounts bear witness to the miracle and possibility of resurrection and not to life beyond resurrection. The one exception is the story of Jesus, where we are allowed to—in fact we must—witness the rest of the story. And what we learn is that resurrection changes everything. It doesn't just bring back the old life in its former, recognizable husk of body.

When Jesus returns in the body, those closest to him no longer recognize him. Mary, stumbling upon him in the garden, mistakes him for the gardener. Two people on the road to Emmaus, his own followers, walk miles in his company and don't recognize him until they welcome him to their table in hospitality. Thomas needs to touch

Jesus' marred hands and side to see him. A group of seven of his most faithful disciples, among them Peter, John, the twin sons of Zebedee, and others, go fishing on the sea of Tiberius and see a stranger on shore. Only later, when the catch is inexplicably abundant, do they decide that the man, now cooking fish on the shore, must be the Jesus they have traveled with for three years.

Clearly, people do not identify the resurrected Jesus as the Jesus they knew and followed. Something about him must be very different. Seemingly, we do not resurrect without carrying some physical change in our body, enough to alter us from recognition by those we love.

So this boy's return leaves us with great, unanswered questions. What was he like? How was his life changed? How was his mother's life changed? We may not be able to answer these questions, but we know a truth from our own lives, from wrestling against the odds, praying in shadowed and darkened rooms, from lying on dead bodies and willing them back. Resurrection never brings people or relationships back the same way. Redemption won't look the way we imagined it would. It might even come long after we have given up on its arrival. We will have to fumble a bit before we recognize it, and we are probably going to call it by the wrong names—names like *failure* and *loss*.

Ultimately when the risen Jesus is recognized, specific actions seem to be the key. Jesus whispers Mary's name, and she sees him. He breaks bread, and the travelers suddenly know their companion on the road. The nets come up impossibly full after the stranger asks about the catch, and John and Peter understand who that man on the beach has to be. Action becomes the moment of recognition. Without enfleshed action, there is no revelation of the miracle of resurrection. To see clearly, we must act.

I sat in a coffee shop with my friend Hal, a man in his eighties, as he confided to me the pivotal point of his life. Hal grew up on a small cattle ranch in Colorado in a culture of hard work and no frills and Christian doctrine as solid as mountain stone. Those mountains were his whole world. But his own attempts to follow the ranching life that he had never questioned went awry, and his ranch failed. He sold it and went to school to become a teacher and a college professor. At fifty, the father of three was fired from his second teaching position. (He had lost the first.) "I went home to break the news to my wife, and I was told that our landlord had just demanded that we move. There I was, fifty years old with no job, no house, and three children." He paused to let his words sink in, and I touched his hand to register my empathy.

Then he said something that I never would have expected: "Dee Dee, I felt so incredibly . . . *free!*"

All those dead dreams forced Hal to build a life from his passions. He was never a rancher at heart, as much as he admired the sturdy and simple life that ranching gave him as a boy. And though he was a creative man with ideas and a passion for cross-cultural living, he was not a high school or college history instructor. Left to his own devices, Hal probably never would have rejected either of those lives. Complete failure had to do that for him.

He ended up pioneering a new business—an innovative travel program that allowed cross-cultural, in-depth tourism—built unconventionally on his best passions. It has been an incredibly successful venture, and he puts his profits into other projects close to his heart, like helping other low-income people to start businesses from their hunches and dreams. He's won a slew of prestigious awards for his philanthropy and efforts toward sustainable business. What I love about his story is not the success. I appreciate how the failures made Hal reconsider who he was. When his endeavors failed, Hal had to scramble and grasp at straws and find his passionate and authentic self.

I think of Margaret, a woman I met only through her spidery handwriting, a one-line note that came with a modest donation to the nonprofit where I worked. I wrote a thank-you. A few years passed. From time to time, another donation would come, always accompanied by a short note. Finally, I received a note saying that Margaret had cancer, and she expected to die within the year. Her news arrived right as I was pregnant with my first child. We were both journeying different, strange, and new paths—she was moving toward death while I was approaching parenthood. Letters and notes began flowing between us more frequently.

When I was birthing Luke, somewhere between the waves of pain and semiconscious fatigue, I thought of Margaret. I thought of the grandmother of a coworker who I knew was dying as well. I wrote the following to Margaret after Luke's birth:

> Never have birth and death come together so closely for me as when I held Luke's tiny body and considered the journey he had taken in the last twenty-four hours. I tried to imagine the change as he experienced it—the pressure pushing him into some strange and completely unknown passage, his body at the mercy of larger forces. He suddenly had to breathe air, not water. He had to get nourishment through his mouth, no longer relying on a connection to me. In his sleep, he flails his hands in the air, startled not to hit the solid, comforting wall of my body. After living only in warm darkness, he experiences light, coolness, and the touch of skin on his own. Nothing could have prepared him for this life, which is, quite simply, unimaginable. Had there been someone else inside watching my child's journey from the womb, she would certainly have seen that process as death, not life. Only when viewed from this side do we call it birth.
>
> Death must be this same complete, unimaginable change of physical state. It too is an inexorable process that seizes us and over which we have no control. Our only choice is to live into it. We only see death from this side, and it is terrifying. But our faith allows us to claim this promise: What appears to be death is a portal to life transformed. People who do not fear death are very dangerous and very free and very bold people.

She wrote back in letters typed by a friend who took her whispered dictation.

Yes, I feel just like newborn Luke when I contemplate my death, so imminent now. I have a host of questions. What will the room look like? Where are the walls? Is there a bus route that goes there? What will be in the fridge? Silly, but I can't shake it. It's the oddest feeling.

The year dragged on, and Margaret got more of a reprieve than expected. We shared more thoughts. In one letter near the end of her life, I wrote the following:

I have been thinking about the fact that Luke really doesn't understand in any significant way the maturation process that is going on in his body, mind, or spirit. He doesn't have any overall view of the world. He is feeling his way, putting it together only by what he can sense. He does this piece by piece—there is so much to make sense of. He takes a tuft of grass in hand and spends five minutes with it. Then he starts examining the loose soil he pulled it from. Then there are trees, squirrels, flowers—each a different shape and color. He touches them all.

Luke examines one object in his hands closely, makes some sense of it, and then moves to the next. But how it fits together—well, after all, don't we spend most of our lives on that and receive few answers?

I have often thought of death as a process that happens to us. Your deliberate and courageous thoughtfulness about it is different. You are, I think, doing something like what Luke is doing as he lives into what it means to be in this world. You are getting pieces, glimpses of this new reality before you. You do not shy from them. You look at them. You think of how to live through them. You know you don't understand them, but you take them all in.

This open-eyed quality is a rare form of courage. I imagine that you are a very honest woman and that you delude yourself very little. I think that when we are in touch with our frailty—the fact that our lives are short and, for the most part, leave fairly small marks on the face of human history—then we are somehow free. We no longer feel ourselves struggling to make some great and final contribution. We are not caught in ego. We enter into something bigger—the great stream of life, of beginnings and endings, carries us. We can let go of our individual selves somehow.

You are, of course, in the final transition toward which you have been living for several years. You need to concentrate on the change itself, but know there is a foundational love holding you, which has never let you go and to whom you are completely beloved.

Margaret taught me about living in her dying. In the face of death, she was able to let go of many things that had defined her and focus instead on what legacy she wished to leave in this broken world. Death made her serious about where her heart was and what she could do in the time she had left.

In the last months of her life, Margaret sent amazing gifts of support to many nonprofits working on world hunger, housing, education, and other social justice issues. After her death, more donations were disbursed. Her life had been spent in a modest clerical career, but she had a very clear sense of how she wanted her resources used. Failure and loss can make us utterly intentional.

Poet Naomi Shihab Nye captures this possibility in her masterful poem "The Art of Disappearing."

When they say Don't I know you?
say no.

When they invite you to the party
remember what parties are like
before answering.

Someone telling you in a loud voice
they once wrote a poem.
Greasy sausage balls on a paper plate.
Then reply.

If they say We should get together
say why?

It's not that you don't love them anymore.
You're trying to remember something
too important to forget.
Trees. The monastery bell at twilight.
Tell them you have a new project.
It will never be finished.

When someone recognizes you in a grocery store
nod briefly and become a cabbage.
When someone you haven't seen in ten years
appears at the door,
don't start singing him all your new songs.
You will never catch up.

Walk around feeling like a leaf.
Know you could tumble any second.
Then decide what to do with your time.

I look back at all the currents of my life, bearing their shadows
and dreams. I contemplate again race, this groaning earth, marriage
and covenant, my children and my parenting, and aging. I put my
hands in the cold, swirling stream of it, remembering all the lovely
and lost things: my grandmother on her farm, *The Other Side*, friends
who have passed over, the agrarian vision of a life that I will probably not have. I peer into the unseeable future, with all its possible
fears and apocalypses—violence, global capitalism, economic faltering, and ecological devastation.

I regard my beloved, who may never escape his visceral struggle
with depression but who is gifted beyond the ordinary as a teacher
and visionary. My son, brilliant and fiery, with his unique wiring for
which this world may not make an easy place. My daughter, so loving
of beauty and empathetic, and therefore fragile. Me, steeped in big
visions but also judgmental and critical of myself. I am vocationally

frustrated, parentally challenged, and even my faith seems stunted compared to past times of spiritual growth.

Nothing is given, and nothing is steadfast.

I find in my journal a small plea, scribbled faintly in the margin several years back: *Here, then, is the harrowing question—God, can you pour more love into me? Can you lift my small, so-human self in your hands?*

God finally answers this question—this prayer. The resurrection rises, with its new, unknown and yet known face. I am now more who I truly am. Suddenly, unexplainably, I am unfathomably in love with this life. This love comes from nowhere, a surge of some Spirit barreling through me. Unaccountably, every small soul whom I encounter seems drenched in humanness, and I cannot stop loving the flesh and frailty of everyone.

For what, after all, is the real path of love and healing? Is it that Will be free from depression, or is it rather that as he has lived within the belly of that capricious demon, he has learned a mercy toward himself, toward me, and toward others that has anchored him, allowing him to pull others to safety? Does the healing come in his freedom from depression, or has the wounding of depression made him a healer? I think the latter.

I extend my hand again and again to meet the hands of others who are different—racially, culturally, class-wise, or how we live in this world. Sometimes those pulls and distrusts have broken our grasp. Sometimes I have hurt them or they me with hard realities and unhealed legacies of pain. But today, I recognize how much we are learning if only we can keep ourselves in the circle together, if we can try it again, straining toward one another and holding nothing back. I watch others do the same, every day going out to bridge the age difference, the class difference, the color difference.

Just for trying, we receive a gift: We find a way of life that is authentic and fits us. Every day presents us with the possibility of some different choice, a new learning. These become generative—it actually creates a new life.

My spiritual director suggested that I learn a little about Saint Thérèse of Lisieux, who died in 1897 of tuberculosis. She was twenty-four.

"I am never touched by the lives of saints," I wanted to reply, but instead, the pleaser in me took the little book that she offered. I left it untouched for months, dreading the eighteenth-century pieties that lay inside.

What leads us into a book we subconsciously resist? Unthinking, I packed it for a retreat. How did this young soul, scooped from pious household to convent at fifteen, who never left her small hometown, get such wisdom? She stared into my midlife eyes, calling me with songs about God's love that sound new. Paraphrased in my journal are these words I wrote to myself in response to reading Thérèse's wisdoms:

> God adores us. God is not standing there, waiting to be pleased with our silly pieties or with our quests, even if we think God commissioned us to those tasks. Your discouragement at inadequacies, your fixations on whether you are good enough—these things block God even as they masquerade as piety. They make us harsh enemies of ourselves. Don't get fixated on what you could not do, become. Every day will offer you again the chance to do small things with great love. Keeping moving in that great love.

That such insights could be sparked by the writings of a woman surrounded by the punitive and pious core of French Catholic asceticism more than a hundred years ago is as incredible as a child coming to a barren woman in Shunem. *Keep moving in love.* This is precisely what we have failed to do. We have pulled our smooth veils of shame over our failures. We have offered the programmed, impossible-to-resist response to the question "How are you?"—"Fine. Good," we say—when our hearts are breaking. We have believed that it is a faithful act to spread trite theologies and rationales over wounds and pretend they do not exist. We believe that to do otherwise is somehow to deny God's ultimate control or goodness.

205

We have walked that tenuous cusp of encouragement and despondency with great uncertainty. What to say? How much to share? If we are honest about our pain, will we cause another to falter? And will our vulnerability bring us healing, or will it simply become eviscerated by spectator pity?

If the child had not come back to life, would the Shunammite woman's story be remembered? Would anyone have wanted to sit next to her in that inscrutable darkness to hear it? I thank those who have had the courage to tell me those *other* stories, the ones not readily recorded. The ones in which the child did not come back to life or not in his recognizable form. I have been helped by that honesty more than by all the cheerful urgings and testimonies to the power of God that I have ever heard. The man who whispers, "I believe that I will never get over losing my daughter." The woman who confided, "If I had it to do over, I would not have had my children." The lifelong pastor, known for his ministry of healing, admits, "I have been completely unable to be a conduit for any spiritual healing to the person I love best in the world." The older member of my community confides, "I expect to spend the rest of my life forgiving my father. I just hope that I can. But I am trying." These are honest witnesses to those things that still lie in their holy rooms, waiting to be redeemed or resurrected.

O woman of Shunem, be your son alive or be he still lying in that holy room, I thank you for the story. Any redemption must always include remembering those children who did not return to life. All my old dreams are passing now, changing. In their place comes this conviction, sturdy and bare as the furnishings of that holy room (lamp, bed, table): Tell the truth about everything—especially the things that go wrong. And find the gratitude in everything, especially in those times that are hard.

There is nothing that cannot be redeemed. Most of all, our whole and human selves.

My daughter called me when I was on retreat for the week, trying to finish the first draft of this manuscript. Her small, young voice mirrored the yearning I also achingly shared for her, but her words were brave and solicitous.

"How is your writing coming, Mommy? What's it about?"

I looked out the window. "It's about how to grow up, what to become as you grow up." *What you can learn as you really try to grow up*, I thought to myself.

"Will it be done soon?"

"Well, here's the good news. It will never be done. But I'm coming home soon. And I will look more like my true self."

Notes

Chapter 1: Prophet, Woman, Holy Room

1. "No Mirrors in My Nana's House." Lyrics and music by Ysaye M. Barnwell, © 1992, Barnwell's Notes Publishing, Washington, DC.

2. Dee Dee Risher, "Singing for My Life," *The Other Side* (July–August 1997), 47.

Chapter 2: Where My People Came From

1. Annette Lareau, *Unequal Childhoods: Class, Race, and Family Life*, 2nd ed. (Berkeley, CA: University of California Press, 2011).

Chapter 8: Life in the Red-Light District

1. Albert Nolan, O.P. "Spiritual Growth and the Option for the Poor." Quoted from a speech given to the Catholic Institute for International Relations, London, on June 29, 1984.

2. Ibid.

3. This quote is often credited to Lilla Watson, possibly originating from a speech given by Watson at the 1985 United Nations Decade for Women Conference in Nairobi. Watson later said that she was "not comfortable being credited for something that had been born of a collective process." Instead, Watson asks that the quote be credited to aboriginal activists in Queensland, Australia, in the 1970s.

4. John McKnight, "Why 'Servanthood' Is Bad," *The Other Side* (November–December 1995).

Chapter 9: Crossing the Rubicon

1. Musimbi Kanyoro, "Living Across the Chasm," *The Other Side* (July–August 2002), 51.

2. Ibid., 51.

Chapter 10: One Wild and Lovely Life

1. Mary Oliver, "The Summer Day," *New and Selected Poems*, Vol. 1 (Boston: Beacon Press, 1992), 94.

2. Dorothy Day, "Peter Maurin: A Poor Man," *Dorothy Day: Selected Writings*, ed. Robert Ellsberg (Ossining, NY: Orbis Books, 2005). Accessed through http://avonhistory.org/bus/curio2.htm.

3. Tracy Kidder, *Mountains Beyond Mountains: The Quest of Dr. Paul Farmer, a Man Who Would Cure the World* (New York: Random House, 2003), 288–9.

4. Dee Dee Risher, "Anonymous Light in Guatemala," *The Other Side* (May–June 1989), 26–7.

5. Ibid., 27.

Chapter 12: The Woodshed of Grace

1. Henry David Thoreau, "Fleets of Butterflies," *The Writings of Henry David Thoreau, Journal, May 1, 1852–February 27, 1853*, ed. Bradford Torrey (Cambridge, MA: The Riverside Press, 1906), 227.

Chapter 13: Bed, Table, Lamp

1. Wendell Berry, "Marriage," *Collected Poems, 1957–1982* (San Francisco: North Point Press, 1985), 71.

Chapter 15: The Second Touch

1. Lareau, *Unequal Childhoods*.

2. Sandra Tsing Loh, "Tales Out of School, *The Atlantic* (March 2008), http://theatlantic.com/magazine/archive/2008/03/tales-out-of-school/306645/.

Chapter 16: Raising Children Across the Divide

1. "Resegregation in America's Schools," an interview with Jonothan Kozol by *National Education Association (NEA) Today*'s Alain Jehlen. November 2005.

2. Erica Frankenberg and Chungmei Lee, "Race in American Public Schools: Rapidly Resegregating School Districts," The Civil Rights Project (Cambridge, MA: Harvard University, August 2002).

3. Kozol, "Resegregation."

4. Rodney Stark, "Antioch as the Social Situation for Matthew's Gospel," *A Social History of the Matthean Community: Cross-Disciplinary Approaches*, ed. David L. Balch (Minneapolis, MN: Augsburg Fortress, 1991).

Chapter 17: This Reeling Earth

1. Wendell Berry, *Harlan Hubbard: Life and Work* (Lexington, KY: The University Press of Kentucky, 1990), 23.

2. Ibid., 97.

3. Mary Oliver, "John Chapman," *American Primitive* (New York: Atlantic-Little, Brown Books, 1983), 25.

Chapter 21: Coming Home to Ourselves

1. Frederick Buechner, *Secrets in the Dark: A Life in Sermons* (New York: HarperCollins, 2006), 212.

Chapter 22: The Door of Authenticity

1. George E. Vaillant, M.D., *Aging Well: Surpising Guideposts to a Happier Life from the Landmark Harvard Study of Adult Development* (New York: Little, Brown, and Company, 2002).

Chapter 23: Finding Shafts of Light

1. Ann Voskamp, *One Thousand Gifts: A Dare to Live Fully Right Where You Are* (Grand Rapids, MI: Zondervan, 2010).

Recommended by

The Academy
for Spiritual Formation®
THE UPPER ROOM

For those who hunger for deep spiritual experience...

The Academy for Spiritual Formation® is an experience of disciplined Christian community emphasizing holistic spirituality—nurturing body, mind, and spirit. The program, a ministry of The Upper Room®, is ecumenical in nature and meant for all those who hunger for a deeper relationship with God, including both lay and clergy. Each Academy fosters spiritual rhythms—of study and prayer, silence and liturgy, solitude and relationship, rest and exercise. With offerings of both Two-Year and Five-Day models, Academy participants rediscover Christianity's rich spiritual heritage through worship, learning, and fellowship. The Academy's commitment to an authentic spirituality promotes balance, inner and outer peace, holy living and justice living—God's shalom.

Faculty trained in the wide breadth of Christian spirituality and practice provide content and guidance at each session of The Academy. Academy faculty presenters come from seminaries, monasteries, spiritual direction ministries, and pastoral ministries or other settings and are from a variety of traditions.

The ACADEMY RECOMMENDS program seeks to highlight content that aligns with the Academy's mission to provide resources and settings where pilgrims encounter the teachings, sustaining practices, and rhythms that foster attentiveness to God's Spirit and therefore help spiritual leaders embody Christ's presence in the world.

Learn more at http://academy.upperroom.org/.

CPSIA information can be obtained
at www.ICGtesting.com
Printed in the USA
BVOW10s2019060616

450973BV00001B/1/P